MONEY FROM ANYWHERE

Also by Pat O'Bryan

Your Portable Empire, How to Make Money Anywhere Doing What You Love

Tne Absolute Beginner's Guide to Internet Wealth: Everything You Need to Know to Create Your Portable Empire

Tne Absolute Beginner's Guide to Internet Wealth, Volume 2

Published by Portable Empire Publishing, Wimberley, Texas
For more information, or to learn how you can publish your book, visit
www.PortableEmpirePublishing.com

Cover Image: © Alexander Hafemann

MONEY FROM ANYWHERE

Pat O'Bryan

with

Dr. Joe Vitale
Marlon Sanders

also with
Connie Ragen Green
Martha Giffen
Tony Laidig
Colin Joss

CONTENTS

AUTHOR'S FOREWORD

If your mind is empty, it is always ready for anything; it is open to everything. In the beginner's mind there are many possibilities; in the expert's mind there are few.
— *from Zen Mind, Beginner's Mind*

November 19, 2010

Welcome to *Money From Anywhere*. This is the book that can take you from wanting and needing money to making money from anywhere you can find Internet access and these days, that's almost anywhere.

As you read, you'll learn how to build your massive passive income home-business and:

How to find and make products that sell!

How to write compelling copy to get your readers to buy!

How to build and keep a laser-targeted list of BUYERS!

How to make money ANYWHERE!

Inner Game Secrets of Attracting Wealth

The title of this book is *Money From Anywhere*. There are two strong reasons for calling it that.

1. It will teach you how to make money from anywhere there is Internet access. That's pretty much anywhere. I can work from my off-the-grid cabin near Terlingua, Texas, which is miles and miles from the nearest civilization in the beautiful Chihuahua desert. It's got solar power, a well, indoor plumbing, and high-speed Internet.

With my iPad and phone I can work from the passenger seat of a car zooming down the highway, as long as I've got a cell phone signal. On a recent trip to California, we were driving through another desert - the Mojave - and in between checking the map for the nearest coffee shop and hotel, I was able to update my blog, launch a new product, and edit articles.

2. It will also teach you how to attract money from anywhere - to set your intention for the amount of money you want to make, and then let the universe fund that intention. It doesn't matter to you where the money comes from. It can come from anywhere.

This concept originated with Napoleon Hill, and I've tested it. It works. You still have to take action. I'm no fan of the "sittin' n wishin'" school of attraction. I've tested that, too. It doesn't work.

However, I've learned that you can set your intention, use the skills and tools available to you, take action, and get exactly what you want- from a completely different source than you expected.

Be open to it.

This book is the culmination of years of learning, teaching, writing and editing.

It started out in 1996 as *Effortless eBooks*. Through the years I've expanded and rewritten it as I learned new strategies and the market changed. I've also attracted some very exciting cowriters, who bring their own illumination to the subject.

Its next incarnation was *The Absolute Beginner's Guide to Internet Wealth*, which was my first published book. Thousands and thousands of people have read and used that book to get their Portable Empire up and running.

Then, in 1998, it was expanded and published by the world's largest nonfiction publisher as *Your Portable Empire, How To Make Money Anywhere Doing What You Love*. That book became my first best-seller and more thousands of people all over the world have used it to break free from their job mentality and create the financial life of their dreams.

One of the things about *Your Portable Empire* that surprised people was how much emphasis I put on your "inner game." Your "outer game" is what you do: create products, build a list, write blog posts, that sort of thing. Your "inner game" is the mindset you bring to those tasks, and to your life.

This new book contains several new chapters on "your inner game."

Your mind has filters. It has to. The amount of data that hits your eyes and ears in each second far exceeds your ability to process it. These filters are a function of your conditioning. When you were a child, your parents and other care givers gave you instructions about what to focus on. Later, schools and jobs continued this programming.

So, your programming, probably up until now, was passive. Your parents probably meant well, but many of the filters you're using unconsciously are out of date and potentially harmful.

Like this one: "We may not be rich, but at least we're honest."

Ever hear that? I sure did.

It's just packed with negative beliefs. "Rich people are dishonest" is the most obvious one. "We're better than rich people, and if we were rich we'd be less honest, and consequently worse people" is also in there.

My goal is to help you identify these limiting beliefs and replace them with beliefs that will help you achieve your own goals- not those of your parents or your teachers or your football coach.

I'm going to help you go from a "passive" inner game to an "active" inner game, where you design the life of your choice.

Your inner game is probably more important than your outer game. Actually, I'll just go ahead and say it: "your inner game is more important than your outer game."

We all know educated, talented people who are failures. We also know less-educated and less-talented people who are successful.

You want to be successful, or you wouldn't be reading this book. Read, and do, the "outer game" stuff. Also read, and do, the "inner game" work. The combination is very effective.

That brings us to the current incarnation of this book, *Money From Anywhere*.

In this book, we're going to look at the "outer game" things you need to know to take advantage of the new information age economy. We're also going to look at the most effective "inner game" strategies and technologies.

They're both important. Sittin' and wishin', regardless of how clear your beliefs are, won't make you successful. All the action in the world won't get you where you're going if your self-talk is still causing you to self-destruct.

The skillful combination of inner game and outer game will get you where you want to go as fast as possible.

FOREWORD TO *THE ABSOLUTE BEGINNERS GUIDE TO INTERNET WEALTH*, SECOND EDITION

It's early May, 2010 as I write this.

Looking at the forward to the original *Absolute Beginner's Guide to Internet Wealth*, I notice that it starts with "It's late August, 2006, as I write this."

In that forward, I talk about how it seems a blur - going from "broke blues musician," to successful Internet Marketer - in two and a half years.

Well, the blur continues. Since I wrote that original book, I've published a second book, *Your Portable Empire - How to Make Money from Anywhere Doing What You Love*, that become an Amazon best-seller. I've created one of the largest and most successful coaching programs on the 'net- Portable Empire Coaching- http://portableempirecoaching.com Some of my students have become successful Internet Marketers themselves, and a few of them contributed to this book. I'm developing software and social networking sites that are targeted to the general public - I've expanded my "niche" to include the galaxy.

And, my Internet Marketing business has grown geometrically. I still practice the basics I teach in this book. I call this the "Portable Empire System." Your Portable Empire is your online business that you can run from anywhere you can get Internet access, and that's just about anywhere these days.

Since 2006, much has changed. Social Networking, especially Twitter and Facebook, have become ubiquitous and essential marketing tools. New hardware, such as the iPad, other tablet computers, and smartphones, have precipitated increased rates of change in the software we use, and the way we deliver our products. In some ways, it's gotten much easier to be an Internet Marketer, especially for Absolute Beginners. In some ways, it's gotten much harder. Large multinational corporations have discovered Internet Marketing, and changed the process just by participating. Google AdWords, and other online advertising services, have grown and proliferated, making it easier to advertise online.

At the same time, the competition for popular keywords has driven a lot of small entrepreneurs to find alternative ways of attracting customers. The FTC has "clarified" its rulings in regard to online advertising in a way that motivated many of us to change the way we use testimonials and add disclaimers to our sales pages. And books.

(Disclaimer - when I talk about things like "you can get rich doing it," I'm speaking from my own experience and observation of my coaching students. I have no idea what YOU can do. Nothing in this book should be misconstrued as a promise of any outcome. I believe in what I teach, and I've watched some of my students use what I teach to build their own Portable Empires. I've also watched some of them sputter, tailspin, and give up. I don't know why some people become successful and some don't. My wish is that you use what I teach to prosper and live a life of freedom. This book comes with no warranties, express or implied.)

Trust me, the basics still work.

You need somebody to sell to and something to sell to them. You can make a good living by solving other people's problems. If you're smart and dedicated, and have good coaching/mentoring, you can get rich doing it.

Imagine that. A business model based on helping others.

I still teach that building your own list and marketing to that list is the most effective way to sell your products. The important thing to remember is that your relationship with your list is the most important asset you own. Make it a two-way street. They'll tell you what their problems are. Solve those problems and sell them the solutions. Also, the definition of "list" has changed to include Twitter, Facebook, and whatever comes next.

That's the Portable Empire System in a nutshell. The rest of this book expands on it. I'll also touch on "Your Inner Game," which is just as important as the metrics of Internet Marketing. Most of the "outer game" failures I've observed could be traced back to a weak "inner game."

Finally, to paraphrase Julia Cameron, "this is a book you do, not a book you just read." I'll try to make it entertaining, but ultimately your success is your responsibility. If you DO what you learn in this book, it can change your life in many ways. If you just read this book, or worse, just put it on the shelf next to the other books you're going to read someday, it won't do you any good at all.

Remember, "if you keep doing what you've done, you'll keep getting what you've gotten."

I'd like to thank: my wife-like girlfriend, Betsy, for her continued patience and support. Dr. Joe Vitale for being a great mentor and a better friend. Our kids for not spending ALL the money. So far. Bill Hibbler for helping me up the first few hills. Craig Perrine, John Carrick, Rodney Bursiel, Elizabeth Lee, and the rest of my friends. You know who you are. Craig Burdett for making the tech stuff work and keeping a sense of humor while doing so. Geoff Hoff for keeping the customers satisfied and reminding me to hit "record."

ORIGINAL FOREWORD

Dr. Joe Vitale

Can anyone–even you–make money online?

Before you answer, consider the following:

I started as an Internet skeptic over 15 (now 20) years ago. I thought the rumors of gold in cyberspace were hype. As usual, I was wrong. I'm living proof. I went from nothing online to being something of a cyberspace celebrity. Google my name and look out. I've got more websites than most people have time to review. I've got more books online than most people read in a lifetime, and the best news of all is that they all make me money, even while I sleep...

...even while I write this foreword.

Maybe you think I'm an exception.

So, you're a skeptic, too?

Well, look at the author of this book. He was a successful musician. By "successful" I mean he had CDs out, he was performing, and people were applauding.

But, he was broke.

I still remember the day he came to my house, red faced in frustration, saying he just wanted to make enough money to pay his fricking rent. (note: I didn't say "fricking")

Today, he is an Internet guru in his own right. He pays his rent just fine. I've seen him splurge on new cars, guitars (including one for me), gadgets and gifts, trips, and more. He learned quickly, took action, and kept cranking out new products. Given that the Internet is a marvelous place to try ideas for virtually nothing, he was able to get up and running almost overnight. Today he's a success, and he's written this book.

You can do it, too.

How?

This book explains it all, step by step. The beautiful thing about the author is that he is articulate, colorful, memorable and caring. He takes his time to be sure you understand the online world. He takes you by the hand and teaches you, from the kindergarten stage on up, how to make money online. Whether you're a newbie or a seasoned nettie, you'll learn from this book.

I'm flattered that Pat asked me to write this introduction for you, but I'm more proud of his success. If he can go from zero to $100,000 (note: way past $100,000) a year, and if I can begin as a skeptic and make a name for myself online, think of what is possible for you. We didn't have this book when we started. You do. You have the edge.

I will be watching for your smoke.

Go for it.

Dr. Joe Vitale is the author of way too many books to list here.

See http://www.MrFire.com

HOW TO USE THIS BOOK

I recommend that you read the whole book once. This will give you an overview of Internet Marketing, and a look at the "inner game" technologies that are available to you.

That should give you an idea of how it all fits together.

This book is composed of "outer game" and "inner game" chapters.

The "outer game" chapters are the ones about choosing your niche, copywriting, affiliate marketing, Internet marketing, etc. Those are the chapters that will teach you what to do to make money from anywhere.

The "inner game" chapters are the ones about how to be. How to get rid of limiting beliefs, become your best friend, and how to embrace success and prosperity in a healthy way.

After you've read the book, go back to the "outer game" chapters.

I suggest you DO those chapters. There are specific instructions and action steps that you can perform right now.

You'll be learning several different approaches to making money from anywhere. Find the one that resonates with you and do that. You'll know it resonates because it will sound obvious and easy.

Return to the "inner game" chapters for inspiration, encouragement, and guidance. Some of them will resonate with you more than others. Those are the ones that are for you.

PROPOSAL: "A NEW AMERICAN DREAM"

A man is rich in proportion to the number of things he can afford to let alone.

— Henry David Thoreau.

When my book, *Your Portable Empire- How To Make Money from Anywhere Doing What You Love*, was published in August, 2007, it was called "The most dangerous book ever."

What made that book dangerous was that, underneath the technical "how-to" Internet Marketing information was a philosophy that the current economic model was terminally broken. The days when you could go to school, go to college, and then get a job that would support you economically for the rest of your life are over.

That philosophy stated that "a job is the least effective way to make money. That if you have a boss, you are a slave. And, it posited that it was past time to free the slaves.

Good bye, American dream.

Good riddance.

It's time for a new American Dream.

Even if such a life would provide you with enough money to live, that's not really living. Far too many people sacrificed their lives for a "McLife." They had a house, a car, a TV set, and - possibly - a 2-week vacation once a year. Hatched 2.5 kids who grew up to do the same thing. Then, after 40 years in a mind-numbing job, they retired. Too old to enjoy the freedom and too many decades removed from the dreams that would make that freedom worth having.

All this worldly wisdom was once the unamiable heresy of
some wise man.

— *Henry David Thoreau*

A friend of mine who worked as a hospice nurse told me that he saw a tragic scene several times in his career: A terminally ill home-hospice patient, looking out the window at the RV that he never got to drive. Just imagine the trips not taken. The scenery undiscovered. The adventures not experienced. And for what?

A house, a car, and a TV set?

That is not living.

In my book, I proposed that almost anybody could make enough money from almost anywhere to support a creative and adventurous lifestyle. My coaching clients are proving it. I get emails regularly from people who have actually USED the information in my book to create the lives of their dreams. You can do it, too - if you WILL do it.

The world has changed.

Before the industrial revolution, each family was a business. Groups of families were villages. There were towns, but the majority of the population was rural. It was entirely possible to trade one of your hens for an equal value in fresh-baked bread. Money, (which is an abstraction - it has no value, but it represents value. It's a lie we all pretend to believe.) wasn't necessary.

You could get your food, beer and wine, and entertainment within a mile or so of where you lived.

Centralized production created the demand for centralized labor. This led to some very shady political maneuvers that drove the peasants (that's us) to the cities, where they could make "a living" working in a factory. This worked out fine for the factory owners and politicians, but was the moment when individual freedom pretty much ended.

Imagine pushing a "fast-forward" button, and watching the world change. You've seen videos of a flower opening- where days of blossoming are telescoped into a few seconds as the rose goes from a bud to a bloom. Imagine that you could see the western hemisphere like that. Watch Detroit, Manchester, Munich and other industrial towns as they grow like serf-devouring monsters in a bad sci-fi movie into mega cities.

Then, as the industrial revolution ends, watch them decay.

That's where we are now on the time line. The industrial revolution is over. Good riddance.

Remember Marx and Engels' comments about the "means of production?" Their complaint was that in the battle between the owners of the means of production and the providers of labor, the power was on the side of the owners.

Until the advent of the Internet, the cost of the means of production was beyond the reach of most people. It cost millions of dollars to build a steel factory or an oil refinery. So, the people with capital invested in the factories and refineries and, to them, labor (that's us) was just a cost of doing business. To make a profit, it is necessary to keep the cost of doing business as low as you can.

In a nutshell, if you produced a dollar worth of value, you HAD to get paid less than a dollar. The difference between what you produced and what you were paid is profit for the company.

That means, to you and me, that as laborers we were in an unequal battle- and we lost it gracefully. We bought the "American Dream" and thought we were winning it. The TV told us that we had it made. Almost. There was always something else to buy to achieve happiness, and it never quite worked, did it? Because there was always one more thing to buy.

Fast forward that tape to a couple of decades ago, and look at the fortunes that were made by kids working out of dorm rooms and garages. Apple computer, Microsoft, Dell, to name a few.

Of that group, Microsoft is the most interesting, because they didn't make anything. Bill Gates "acquired" an existing operating system and somehow persuaded IBM and other computer manufacturers to install it on the computers they manufactured. It didn't work very well, and subsequent "improvements" to that code worked equally poorly, or not at all. Remember Windows Millenium?

It didn't matter. It worked well enough to usher in a complete and total economic revolution.

Gates acquired riches that leave one breathless, and he did by recognizing the new paradigm. The industrial revolution is over, and we have entered a new revolution.

IBM had to make millions of computers one at a time. Make one, sell one. Gates acquired code once, and sold it millions of times.

That one event changed everything. Forever.

That success of that event, which put a computer on every desk and in every backpack in the western world, killed the American dream dead, and put the final nail in the coffin of the industrial revolution.

The line between labor and capital has disappeared.

You can slope over to Best Buy and get the means of production for less than $500.

The most expensive personal computer I've heard of belongs to Armand Morin. He claims to have paid $8,500 for it, and I believe him.

That sounds like a lot of money, but it wouldn't buy the door on a steel factory. It wouldn't pay for the first pipe in an oil refinery. And he'll make millions of dollars a year with it.

And, honestly, that computer won't do a thing that the $500 computer won't do. It may do it marginally faster, and I suspect the graphics are stunning- but, with a $500 computer and some rudimentary knowledge of Internet Marketing, you can replace that factory job.

Good thing, too. The factory jobs are pretty much gone, aren't they? Unless you speak Chinese or whatever they speak in India and are willing to work for a dollar a day.

If you're good, you can make more money than the manager of that factory used to make- and do it in less than an hour a day. From a coffee shop in Paris. Or a beach in Mexico.

> *Do not worry if you have built your castles in the air. They are where they should be. Now put the foundations under them.*
>
> *— Henry David Thoreau*

Last night, I was talking to my son and his girlfriend. The topic turned to: "what about all the people who just want a job?"

Incredulous, I asked them to explain.

"Some people just want a job. They want to be told what to do, and do it in exchange for enough money to live on."

As hard as that is for me to believe, it must be true. The world is full of people who have let their dreams die and abdicated responsibility for their own lives. That's what having a "job" means to me.

It can't be for the security. There's much more security in owning your own online business than there is in working for someone else. If you work for yourself, you know the boss is going to look out for you. If you work for someone else, you're just an expense.

Profit = income – expenses.

The boss is looking out for profit, or he'll lose his job. Or his business. He can't look out for you.

Normally, I'm not a big fan of social Darwinism. I've noticed that most of the proponents of social Darwinism have rich daddies. However, in this case, I don't see any options.

Adapt or die.

Personally, I'd love to live in a country that guaranteed "the basics" to all its citizens. So much of the wealth of a nation should, in my opinion, belong to the citizens of that nation. Oil, minerals, etc., in a perfect world, would belong to all, and the income from that wealth should be divided among the citizens of the nation.

I'd cheerfully do without a few wars of conquest, bridges to nowhere, and subsidies to large corporations to make that happen.

However, it ain't gonna happen. I'll leave it to you to figure out why.

My theory is that if we all had "the basics" as a basic right- food, shelter, health care, clean water, electricity, Internet access, to start with- then you could make a case for social Darwinism. Survival of the fittest.

I understand why the trust fund crowd is against this. It would increase the competition. If one person is struggling to just pay the rent and another is living rent-free thanks to mom and dad, and those two people are competing against each other, it's just not a fair game.

I'd love to see the playing field leveled. Then, we'd see who would prosper. I predict the results would be surprising.

The people who stand to lose the most from a level playing field also control the information delivery services. If you're poor, uneducated and uninformed, the odds are that you get your information from popular news. Somehow, news makes the case that leveling the playing field would be bad for you. They use high-impact words like "socialism," Marxism, and UnAmerican - and, if you're in that group, you don't know what those words mean. You haven't read the *Communist Manifesto*. You haven't really explored the socialist countries that are actually kicking the United States' ass in terms of quality of life for the citizens. And, you're probably not reading this.

They say it. You believe it. That settles it. You go to bed with a comfortable sense of righteous outrage and wake up still a slave.

It's amazingly effective propaganda, and it's not going to change.

So, odds are that unless you happen to have a trust fund, you're going to have to come up with enough money to provide your own basic needs before you can work on the fun stuff- like investments, self-actualization, culture, spirituality.

Above, I pointed out that the difference between the value of what you produced and what you got paid to produce it equals profit to the company.

In the new economy, you have the freedom to receive the entire value of what you produce. That can be very good news.

The framework of what I call the Portable Empire System is based on solving problems. People will pay for the solutions to their problems.

Some people have the problem of being bored. If you can entertain them, they will make you ridiculously rich. That's why sports stars, actors and musicians can make the kinds of salaries they make.

Johnny Depp, as Captain Jack Sparrow, was underpaid- even though he makes tens of millions of dollars per picture - because he entertained millions of people. Lady Gaga, Madonna, Dr. Dre, the Beatles, U2, Tiger Woods, Tony Romo – you've got your own list, I'm sure - are making exactly what they're worth. They sell tickets. They create wealth.

The cover band at the local bar, and the actors in the community theater are making exactly what they're worth, too.

We can't all be Johnny Depp.

Who are you? That's the question. What value do you bring to the world?

What problems can you solve?

Your income, if you choose to maximize it, will represent the value of the problems you can solve multiplied by the number of people you help.

Some people have the problem of being fat, and they'd rather be thin.

Some people have the problem of not having money, and they'd rather have some.

Some people have the problem of not being clear about spirituality, and are seeking clarity.

Acceptance. Self image. Health. Sports. There is not, and never will be, a lack of problems. People will pay you for a solution to their problem.

That's the information economy, and it's the economy we live in now.

I don't know where the jobs are in this economy, and I don't know why you'd want one.

With a laptop computer, some training- which is available online, and less than fifty bucks a month for operating capital, you can make more money than most jobs will pay- and you can do it wherever you want, whenever you want, and have time to actually live.

If that doesn't appeal to you, I recommend that you learn Chinese and start packing.

> *As you simplify your life, the laws of the universe will be simpler; solitude will not be solitude, poverty will not be poverty, nor weakness weakness.*
>
> — *Henry David Thoreau*

Before we leave this subject, I'd like to talk about my friends in Terlingua. Some of them are rich. Almost all of them are wealthy- even the ones who don't have any money. One of the wealthiest guys I know lives in a 400 square foot geodesic dome in the desert. He's my nearest neighbor.

He'll help you out for $10/hour if he likes you. If he's not busy watching a sunset or playing with his pet roadrunner. Or, tooling about the desert in his old jeep.

You can buy land for $80/acre in the desert near Big Bend National Park. I've done it. So have hundreds of other people. Some of them are living in domes or yurts. Others are living in RVs and travel trailers. Some have salvaged old railroad cars or shipping containers and converted them into shelter - and some of them are pretty comfy.

Since the government isn't going to provide the basics, these people just redefined what "the basics" means to them and provide it for themselves.

What do they really need?

Shelter, water, food, and some of the most inspirational scenery in the world seems to do it for them. By decreasing consumption and creating their own entertainment they're able to live on a couple of hundred dollars a month. For another hundred, they can get Internet access and a land-line telephone. Even at $10 per hour that represents very little time spent on earning the money to live, and leaves a whole lot of time for living.

If everybody lived like they do, it would be the end of some things that have long outlived their usefulness. Oil companies and electric utilities, for example. We'd have to find new reasons to go to war, wouldn't we? Or we could just skip the war part completely.

Most of them have spent their time in corporate America. They've had jobs. They took a cold, hard look at the "American Dream," and rejected it. At least, they've rejected the prepackaged "American Dream." The McLife. They turned their back on the plastic imitation life and are living real ones.

Having the freedom and resources to do exactly what you want to do when you want to do it is a pretty good definition of wealth.

So, once you decide what it is that you really want from life, you'll know how much money you need. Making that decision can be tough. I'm still struggling with it myself. In a world of infinite options, and infinite potential lives, how do you choose the one life that's right for you?

I'm still working on that, but I'm sure that being a slave won't make you free.

If you'd like to learn more about the Portable Empire System, and how to start and run your own online business, go tohttp://portableempirecoaching.com.

Finally, I'd like to propose a new American Dream.

Free people, living where they want and doing what they want, when they want. Imagine a nation of people like that. Imagine living like that.

That would indeed be a land of the free and the home of the brave. Let's make it real.

ATTRACT $175,000 TODAY

Dr. Joe Vitale

In 1931 Vash Young inherited a fortune. This was during the Great Depression in the USA when much of the country lost jobs, savings, hopes, dreams, and more. Young was so grateful for his inherited fortune that he spent his entire life sharing it.

Last week I inherited his fortune.

It was strange, unexpected, and yet incredible.

I didn't know Young before last week, though I had heard of his fortune.

I never imagined he would pass it on to me.

I'm grateful for it, of course.

Who wouldn't be?

And I'm now going to share that fortune with you.

Let me explain.

A friend of mine in the Miracles Coaching program told me about an old book he found that he thought I might like. But he couldn't recall the title or author. He was obviously moved by the book. I'm a bookaholic, so I was interested, even without all the details. I asked him to send me the book's info when he came across it. I didn't think any more about it.

But last week my friend sent me a package. Inside was the mysterious book. The title is *A Fortune to Share*. The author was Vash Young. I had never heard of the book or the author. Since I was busy with projects, such as scheduling the launch of my new audio program (The Abundance Paradigm), and already had fifteen books to read either on my iPad or my desk, I just put the book aside. It would have to wait.

But the book wouldn't wait.

Something about it called me to it. Maybe because the book was from 1931 and looked like a lost gem in self-help and self-improvement; maybe because I love success literature and this title seemed like it was from that category; maybe because I hoped the author had been a friend of a man I wrote about from that era, Bruce Barton, in my book *The Seven Lost Secrets of Success*; maybe because the author put a spell on the book. I don't know. But before I knew it, everything else got pushed aside and I started reading *A Fortune to Share*.

Within minutes, I was captivated.

The book is written in the first person, with the author talking to me about his fortune and how it changed his life. The old Young of poverty and reckless living was gone; the new Young was now so rich that even the Great Depression couldn't touch him.

His mission became the life-long quest to share his fortune with others.

I was riveted.

Young explained that you own a factory. Most of the time you make junk in that factory. As a result, no one buys from you. No wonder you were broke and struggling. No wonder life looked bleak. Your factory wasn't producing what anyone wanted.

He went on to explain that the same factory could make gold.

Gold?

How?

In your mind.

In your mind!

As it turns out, the fortune Young inherited was the gold inside himself: his ability to control his thoughts, beliefs, moods, and attitude. He could let the factory of his mind create a life that was miserable, or he could take charge of that factory and get it producing new thoughts, beliefs, moods and attitude that he and others would want.

He inherited a mental fortune.

As long as Young accepted his fortune and shared it, everything he wanted would come his way, and without trying to make it happen.

Young literally did attract a financial fortune (he sold over $80,000,000 in life insurance) due to his discovery and his sharing. He went from a life of go-getting to a life of go-giving. (He later wrote a book titled *The Go-Giver*.) The more he gave, the more he attracted. His mission truly became one of sharing the mental fortune inside himself to awaken your own understanding that you have a mental fortune inside you, too.

While it's easy to wish that Young's fortune was all cash and he shared it by writing checks (which he often did, just not to you or me), what he actually gave us is something far more valuable: he pointed out you have a cash-making machine in your head.

In short, we attract "junk" when we think from selfishness and fear; we attract "gold" when we think and act with love.

A Fortune to Share contains much more information, and many wonderful stories. It's a hypnotic read. Breezy. Easy. Fast. It also delivers some unforgettable wisdom, such as:

"Any experience can be transformed into something of value."

"Prosperity can not be built on fear!"

For a long time, Young would hold "Trouble Day" every Saturday. He would let anyone walk into his office, dump their troubles on him, and then Young would do his best to help the troubled soul with his philosophy, and often with money.

In talking to an unemployed man one day, Young tells him, "You haven't been unemployed all these months, you have been working for the wrong boss. You have been working for failure, discouragement, fear and worry and the sad part of it is that there has been no salary for your labors. You seem to be destitute, but I am going to tell you how to become rich overnight. I want you to deposit the following thoughts in your mental bank tonight: 'I am not afraid – I am a success, not a failure – I have an inexhaustible supply of courage, energy, confidence and perseverance.'"

Young helps the man out with a suit of clothes and a little money, and reminds him to draw on his new mental bank account when he needs it.

Within a week, the man has a job he loves.

Young's first book was so sincere, helpful and timely that it became a national bestseller. He followed it with several others (which I have yet to read but eagerly await), including *The Go-Giver*, *Be Kind to Yourself*, and *Let's Start Over Again*. All were bestsellers. All were booster rockets for a weary country suffering during the Great Depression of the 1930s. When Young was in his seventies in 1959, he wrote a final book summing up his philosophy of life, called *Fortunes For All*.

I found *Fortunes For All* and read it. Loved it, too. On the cover the publisher says, "Let Vash Young show you that your mind is worth $175,000 or more!"

How can your mind bring you $175,000?

Here's the secret:

Young explains that instead of asking, "How can we have more?" we should ask, "How can we be more?"

He then invites you to try an experiment:

"Go off by yourself with a pad and pencil and write out your own ticket for a happy and successful life. By that I mean put down all of the things you would like to have or be."

He adds, "After imagining every wish has been granted, then go one step further. Start in being the ideal person you think you would be if you had everything your way."

Young's philosophy of fortune basically said that once you began to be that happy, successful person now, then you would naturally attract all you wanted from the being.

Sounds a whole lot like step four in my book, The Attractor Factor, and step five in my book *Attract Money Now*, where I suggest you "Nevillize" a goal to help bring it into reality.

In other words, feel what it would be like to already have the thing you want or be the person you long to be. Feel it now.

But Young is also wanting you to be something greater than a satisfied person. He wants you to embody the traits of — dare I say it — God.

Decades ago in Houston I gave a talk where I encouraged people to think like God. I said God wouldn't think in terms of lack and limitation. Why should you?

But Young wants you to act like God, meaning live love, compassion, forgiveness and all the other positive, enlightened states that a God would have.

Be God.

Young was a great believer in taking action, too.

A chapter on selling in *Fortunes For All* proves that he sold such a staggering amount of life insurance by focusing on giving, thinking of others over himself, and following his being principle. But he also took non-stop action. Even when Young was on jury duty for three weeks, he still held the sales record for the month. How? He kept taking action.

All of this is so inspiring and powerful that I wish Vash Young was still alive so I could thank him in person. But I've inherited his fortune. And I'm sharing it with you. I'm hoping you will now share it with others, too.

Take control of your mind and you can live a life of magic and miracles — a life of good fortune.

It's Vash Young's inheritance.

It's my inheritance.

And now it's yours.

What do you think, anyway?

What is your factory producing?

Who's the boss of your own mind?

Who are you being?

Enjoy your new fortune.

Dr. Joe Vitale is famous for creating Hypnotic Writing and Miracles Coaching, but he's also written 53 books (such as *The Attractor Factor*), appeared in 13 movies (such as the hit *The Secret*), and has bestselling audios (such as *The Secret to Attracting Money*) and more.

His main website is http://www.joevitale.com. Read his book *Attract Money Now* for free at http://www.attractmoneynow.com

STEP BY STEP FROM SCRATCH GAME PLAN TO BUILD A TRUE SEMI-AUTO PILOTED INTERNET BUSINESS (OR EVEN AN EMPIRE)

Marlon Sanders

So you wanna start from scratch and stick some dough in your bank account.

Hey, I don't blame ya. You got bills to pay, a retirement to worry about. A mortgage payment. A car payment.

Whew! That doesn't even include kids, gas and clothes. No wonder you wanna bring in some dough part time and possibly even full time on the Net.

I started in this business way, way, way back on AOL and Compuserve. I'd run a little freebie classified ad offering a report.

People would email me and I'd hand email them back. Things weren't very automated back then and they've thankfully come a very long ways.

But get this: I use the SAME formula today as I did back then and you can too.

I started out of a tiny 600 square foot apartment, where I barely had any room for books or courses.

I had a little white wooden press board desk my friend Kelli gave me.

I had a 386 computer I bought from the Dax mail order catalog not to mention the dot-matrix computer. I must say I'm VERY happy to have a faster computer today.

If you can write or you can talk, you might find this is the perfect business for you.

Now, I'm known as the "King of Step-By-Step Internet Marketing Training."

So in a minute, I'm going to lay some step-by-step goodness on you to prove and demonstrate I really AM the King.

So what took me from that tiny 600 square foot apartment to world travel, highly prestigious speaking engagements around the world and even to having the organization for genius folks (Mensa) put one of my products in their online catalog?

What allowed me to bring in 100's of thousands of dollars a year like I have for years now while working so little time in a day it's almost embarrassing? (I consider 30 minutes to an hour a good day's work).

The answer is what I dubbed many years *The Amazing Formula That Sells Products Like Crazy.*

See, either you trade products for dollars or you trade time for dollars.

I'd a lot rather trade products, so I can spend MY time the way I wanna spend it.

Here's my little step-by-step System for doing that:

Step One: Find a group of people who are passionate and buy lots of stuff, especially expensive stuff.

a. Given the choice of selling to broke people or people with money, it's better to sell to people with money!

b. Find people who not only spend money but spend it over and over and over.

Here's an example: Golfers.

Do you golf or know anyone who does? Chances are they have golf equipment, gloves, eBooks on how to golf, books, cd's or courses on it, and so forth.

Avid golfers just can't get enough stuff that will help them golf better! And they're willing to pay good money to improve their game.

Oh, they buy over and over and over.

Or take my dad.

He builds model airplanes...you know, the kind you fly on remote control. Talk about an expensive hobby! Those planes cost $1,000 and $2,000 each for the kits!

And then there are plans you can buy, videos, DVD's – all kinds of stuff.

Step Two: Look at what the people BUY and spend money on over and over.

a. All things being equal, it's better to sell 'em something similar to what they're already buying.

No use reinventing the wheel too much.

b. Study the web sites they go to, blogs they read and the forums they go to.

(Side note: If you don't have my Promo Dashboard and Product Dashboard, they show you step by step how to do this. Those 2 are part of what I call my Basics Pack for newbies to get up and running super quick with a minimum of time spent trying to figure stuff out. It's the ultimate in step-by-step simplicity)

Step three: Look at what people buy to START with and then what they buy over and over or things they buy that are more expensive.

We call this the marketing funnel.

Typically, a new customer buys something cheap. Then they buy things that are more expensive.

You want to have a little funnel of stuff that becomes more expensive as they go along.

Step four: Create a freebie to get people on your email list.

I did this way back in the AOL days by running classified ads. But I had to send the reports or freebies by hand. Today a thing called an autoresponder does it for you.

Step five: Send 2-5 emails a week

Once you get people on your email list, send offers for affiliate products until you have your own. See, you can sell OTHER people's products and get a commission for doing so.

If you want to see what my affiliate program looks like, just go to http://getyourprofits.com and you can scope it all out.

Here's the thing: Even if you only have 10 people on your email list, you need to start sending emails and learn how to write emails that get people to click.

That's really key.

One of my friends did that. And when he had 10 people on his list, one of 'em bought his $300 product!

He started sending out daily emails and it worked like a charm. It works for me also and many of my friends. And I'm pretty sure that if you follow this formula, it'll work for YOU also.

Now, I like to lead with cheap offers. Usually under $100 and sometimes under $10. But it really depends on your list.

Step six: Mix in content, entertainment and good stuff with your promotional emails.

Do NOT send all pitches. Add in links to videos or podcasts. Or do little articles that have content.

Make people WANT to stay on your list and read your emails.

Step seven: Once people buy, sell 'em more expensive stuff!

You know, move 'em up your funnel.

Regularly create little videos, emails, podcasts or other forms of content or entertaining things that your customers will love and send 'em out.

Here's the AUTOPILOT part:

Once you get emails that work, you just stick 'em in your autoresponder and the sales happen automagically!

This is the greatest feeling in the world.

You'll be so jazzed, pumped and excited when you realize you don't have to even show up for work and you'll STILL have sales coming in and money being deposited in your bank account.

This is what's so freaking awesome about Internet marketing.

Now, let's summarize my 7-step Game plan for you:

Step One: Find a group of people who are passionate and buy lots of stuff, especially expensive stuff.

Step Two: Look at what the people BUY and spend money on over and over.

Step Three: Look at what people buy to START with and then what they over and over or things they buy that are more expensive.

Step Four: Create a freebie to get people on your email list.

Step Five: Send 2-5 emails a week.

Step Six: Mix in content, entertainment and good stuff with your promotional emails.

Step Seven: Once people buy, sell 'em more expensive stuff!

Marlon Sanders is the author of *The Amazing Formula That Sells Products Like Crazy* and the KING of Step-By-Step Internet Marketing.

To get on his killer eZine list, to get cheat sheets and all kinds of other goodies every Saturday and during the week, to get simple, to-the-point Internet marketing know that works real world without all the hype, go to: http://www.marlonsnews.com and subscribe.

GETTING STARTED — CHOOSING YOUR NICHE

The ability to convert ideas to things is the secret of outward success.

— Henry Ward Beecher

There are three main components to keep in mind when you're building your Portable Empire:

Building your list

Building your relationship with your list

Making products and selling them to your list, and through Joint Venture and affiliate arrangements, Social Media, advertising, Public Relations, and other methods, to the universe.

Let's talk about choosing your niche. This is the playground where you're going to play - so keep it interesting and fun.

According to the Merriam-Webster dictionary, niche means:

a: a place, employment, status or activity for which a person or thing is best fitted <finally found her niche> b: a habitat supplying the factors necessary for the existence of an organism or species c: the ecological role of an organism in a community especially in regard to food consumption d: a specialized market

When we talk about our "niche" in Internet Marketing, we're referring to d: a specialized market," although the other definitions are relevant.

There are two philosophies, at least, that address choosing your niche.

The first is based on metrics. For example, you can use Google's search engine, Google's keyword tool, alexis.com, and Spyfu.com to analyze what people are searching for, and with that information extrapolate what problems they're trying to solve. With that information, you can create a solution to these problems and market it.

Fortunes have been made using this method.

The second is the one I recommend in the original *Absolute Beginners Guide* where you choose a topic that you're 1) interested in and 2) knowledgeable about. Then, you use the tools above to discover whether or not there is enough demand in that niche to justify your business. If you're passionate and knowledgeable about underwater basket weaving, but only four people a month search Google for those keywords, what you have is a hobby. If you're passionate about iPads (right now), and eleventy-billion people are searching Google for iPad related information, you're going to be competing with some pretty big dogs. I'd recommend something in the middle.

My thinking has changed in the last four years when it comes to choosing niches. Originally, I advised my readers to carefully choose one niche, and make sure it was something you were interested in. I still teach that.

However, over time I've developed a suspicion that confining yourself to a niche is an unnecessary limitation.

For example, my main two niches are 1) teaching Internet Marketing to beginning marketers and 2) providing inspirational "inner game" material to "new age" thinkers. I'm still making the majority of my income from those two niches.

Recently, I've added "software developer" to my title, and the first product we're developing will be useful for anybody who uses the Internet. You can try it for free at http://videolinkgenerator.com.

I've also developed a social networking site, MommyGalaxy.com, that serves people outside my niches. And, with Dr. Joe Vitale and a small group of others, I'm creating information projects for help with weightloss.

I call my new projects "mainstreaming." By that, I mean that I'm creating solutions for the general public, independent of the limitations of "niche."

When you're first starting out, I recommend you stick with my original recommendations.

Here's how I put it in the original *Absolute Beginner's Guide*:

It's important to target all of your efforts to one specific, specialized market. To develop a large, loyal list of subscribers, you need to offer a solution to a problem that is shared by a large group of people.

Over time, one of your most valuable possessions will be your list of people who are not only interested in the solution to their problems, but will also pay you for those solutions. (Note- actually, this is a function of the relationship you build with the PEOPLE on that list. A phone book is a large list. It's useless for marketing. Make your list a two-way street.)

If you choose your niche wisely, it will be deep enough to include lot of related, linear problems. For example, my niche is education, specifically in the area of Internet Marketing for beginners.

That's a big playground. I can talk about the mind set of success, the inner game of marketing, how to create a PDF file, video editing, and hundreds of other related topics. I can provide the information as an eBook, and audio download, a CD, streaming video, or a DVD.

You might want to jot this down: "Every problem is a product."

As my customer solves one problem- hopefully with a solution they buy from me- that leads them to the next problem. (That's what I mean by linear.)

My job is to make sure they know about the problem, and make it easy for them to buy the solution from me. At that point, the client will weigh how important the problem is to them, how long it would take them to solve it on their own, and hopefully purchase the solution.

Over time, I've created a lot of solutions. As I solve each problem for myself, I turn that solution into a product.

To the people who are behind us on the learning curve, we're the experts.

I've left a trail of solutions, and gathered a list of people who are on the same journey as I am. This is how you create multiple streams of passive income.

(Note - recently, on a coaching UnWebinar, I showed my coaching students my 1shoppingcart sales report for the month. The point I made to them was that it was a long report. Some products contribute more income at any given time than others, but the cumulative effect of marketing a LOT of products is what creates the bottom line. Your goal is to create multiple streams of passive income by solving lots of problems and marketing the solutions.) You can find out more about that coaching program at http://portableempirecoaching. com

As you read the instructions below for choosing a niche, keep that in mind.

Be sure to pick a niche that has a long learning curve, with lots of fun problems.

Let's take this to the real world.

One of the best tools for communicating with your subscribers is a blog. Mine is at http://patobryan.com/blog.

Recently, one of my coaching clients asked:

Could you please explain how you coach people to success? I have been down this road before trying to come up with a product to solve a problem. I didn't come up with anything! I don't have a clue when coming up with a product...Do you have a specific process to come up with profitable ideas? I hope so, I need the process you go through.

I responded:

I suspect that you're not the only one asking this question. As a matter of fact, my wife-like girlfriend, Betsy, and I were just talking about this over dinner. She's struggling with the same problem.

I think we can sort this out.

First, you need to chunk the question down and simplify it. Right now, the problem I'd like to solve is breast cancer - a very dear friend is battling this demon, and I've lost several loved ones to it. Another problem I'd like to solve is political - I'm afraid Ike was right when he warned us to beware the military-industrial complex. Then, there's hunger, homelessness, global warming, and the fact that there's not a real first-class Mexican Food restaurant in Wimberley, Texas.

Realistically, I'm not an oncologist, a political scientist, social scientist, or first-class Mexican Food chef. We need to find problems we can actually solve, and hopefully in a niche that we can stay interested in.

To me, that's the real danger - finding a niche that's profitable but boring. I think it's important to find a niche about which you're passionate.

For example, I'm passionate about self-actualization, and I don't think that's something you can achieve working 40 hours a week at a job you don't love. I think humans were created in God's image, and He/She didn't intend for us to spend our brief time on this spinning globe in mind-numbing tedium. I'm convinced that we're living in an infinite universe, and that there are enough resources for everyone. My solution is the "Portable Empire" system, which allows you to travel, think, meditate, and grow to your full potential without having to punch a clock.

So, when I'm looking for a problem to solve, I limit my search to the niche of "Your Portable Empire."

That simplifies the problem, and also simplifies finding the solution. I promote seminars, videos, audios and eBooks that teach people to create multiple streams of passive income.

A lot of my products start out as conversations with my coaching students. It's important to have a dialogue with your customers. They'll tell you what they want. This is very useful information.

STEP ONE IS TO IDENTIFY YOUR NICHE

The best way to predict the future is to invent it.

— *Alan Kay*

How do you do that? You need to find a subject that you're 1) passionate about, 2) knowledgeable about, and 3) is broad enough to have a large customer base.

In my case, I'm passionate about freedom - and you need financial freedom to acquire intellectual freedom and freedom of mobility. I'm knowledgeable about the subject - I make a healthy six-figure income doing what I teach, and finally, there are more than enough people interested in the subject to make it profitable for me.

One way to work your way through the niche-finding problem is to take a piece of paper and draw a line down the middle. On one side, write down all the subjects you're knowledgeable about. Take some time with this- you know a lot more than you think you do.

Then, in the second column, make a similar list of things you're passionate about. PASSIONATE! Not just interested.

Then, see what turns up in both columns. On another sheet of paper, make a list of just the things that are in both columns, with the most fascinating (to you) subject first, the next most fascinating subject second, and so on.

Now, starting with the most interesting subject, do a Google search to see who else is marketing to your future customers, and to confirm that these customers actually exist.

If you turn up a blank, or just a few results, go to the next one. Just because you're passionate about competitive stamp collecting doesn't mean it's a good business. Call that a hobby and move on.

If your Google search turns up page after page of commercial sites- congratulations! You've just identified your future Joint Venture partners. You've found your niche.

Now, let's say you're the kind of person who plays 18 holes of golf every morning, and another 18 every evening. You've got zirconium encrusted drivers and a putter that's been blessed by three popes. Your golf cart has a hemi. Your wife would like you to kindly shut up about golf, because that's all you ever talk about.

You're a golf nut.

Now, let's also postulate that you've spent a few years reading every book you can get your hands on about golf, studied with Tiger Woods, and the local golf pro asks you for advice.

You're a golf expert.

You do a Google search on "golf" and discover that there are millions of people marketing to golfers.

You're in luck.

Your niche is golf.

(Note: Now, there are more tools available to allow you to learn much more about a prospective niche. Google keyword tool (Google it) will tell you how many searches your keywords are getting a month, and where those searches are coming from. Http://spyfu.com will tell you how many people are paying for online advertising for those keywords and where their websites are. This is great to know- you can estimate the cost of doing business in that niche, and see what your competitors are doing.)

Now, to monetize your niche, you need to find out what pressing problems golfers are having and provide them with a solution. You want to identify a problem that really, really hurts them. I live on a golf course, but the last golf course I played on had a little windmill, and I was still in Junior High School at the time, so I'm going to wing it here ...

Do they slice? Do they get tired on hole 17? Hole 3? Is their stance too wide? Are their pants too tight? Have they lost their balls?

How do you find out what THE pressing problem is for golfers today?

Back to Google! (Note: since I wrote this, Twitter and Facebook have become powerful tools for data mining. In addition to searching on Google, search on Twitter and Facebook, too.)

Do a search on "golf forum."

There should be plenty. Join them. Lurk. Read the posts.

I do this with "newbie" Internet forums, including the one I own, MilagroWorld (http://milagroworld.com/forums).

It's a gold mine. Somebody will post a question, several people will join the conversation, mentioning that they've had the same problem. Somebody will post a wrong answer.

Gold mine. Home run. Hole in one.

So, hang out in the forums and identify the one biggest problem that golfers have. Obviously, this will work in any niche.

Sell them the solution.

Initially, you'll probably frame your solution as an eBook. They're free to make, free (http://clickbank.com) to deliver and sell, and work while you're sleeping.

You may discover an olde Scottish tome that is in the public domain that is just chock full of golfing wisdom. Turn that sucker into a PDF, and sell it. See Tony Laidig's chapter below for how to do that.

(Note: some word-processing programs will automatically export your documents as PDF files, which is still the most popular eBook format. I use Open Office, which is a free office suite, to create mine. Http://openoffice.org. Also, Kindle readers, iPads, etc. are changing the way we deliver eBooks. They all have their own opinions about how an eBook should be delivered. I recommend offering your products in as many formats as you can. Make it easy for your customers to buy from you.)

Remember, we're selling information. You can also package the information as an audio MP3 or a video. You may want to consider investing in Camtasia: http://techsmith.com/camtasia.asp.

(In my original book, I discuss the fact that the Internet just isn't fast enough to deliver streaming video. That was true in 2006. We've come a long way. Today, you can easily stream video, even on the 3G network that iPhones and iPads use. You'll want to offer your video in several formats - Flash, for example, doesn't work with Apple products (at the time I'm writing this.) That may change. And yet, Flash is still a popular video format for other platforms.

(If you'd like to market CDs or DVDs, I recommend Kunaki: http://kunaki.com. At this time, they're the best deal I know of and the most dependable service for CD and DVD product fulfilment.)

If your niche is golf, you've got a great niche because it has a lot of very interesting, linear problems.

You could create an "Introduction to Golfing," and then an eBook on how to choose the right golf clubs. Follow that up with "27 Things to Ask Your Golf Pro," "Reports from the World's Best Golf Courses" would be my next choice - and could lead to a nice tax-deductible research vacation.

Get the picture?

(Note: remember, this is a book you DO. There are a lot of action points in the previous chapter. Take a break and DO them. I'll wait.)

HOW TO CREATE VALUABLE INFORMATION PRODUCTS AUTOMATICALLY

Everything you can imagine is real.

— *Pablo Picasso*

You hear it all the time, don't you? "I've got this great idea for an eBook; I just don't know how to write it." Or, "I've been working on my product for months, but I just can't seem to finish it."

I've talked to potential authors who have spent years struggling to write their first eBook!

What if I could show you how to write an interesting and valuable eBook instantly and effortlessly? Would you be interested?

One of my favorite images in American Literature is the young Tom Sawyer, who was commanded to whitewash a fence. It was a boring, tedious job, and he really didn't want to do it.

Knowing that if you want something other than the obvious to happen you have to do something other than the obvious, Tom pretended to have so much fun whitewashing that fence that other boys literally begged him to let them do it.

I've taken Tom's approach to fence painting and applied it to writing eBooks.

WHY WRITE AN EBOOK?

Happiness is not in the mere possession of money; it lies in the joy of achievement, in the thrill of creative effort.
— Franklin Roosevelt:

There are several good reasons to become an eBook author.

1. Money. Information is big business. You can create a product once and sell it thousands or millions of times. Every aspect of the process can be automated except the actual writing - and with the tricks I'm about to show you, even the writing will be easy and painless.

2. Build Your List. Every Internet Marketer knows that "the gold is in your list." I've added thousands of names to my mailing list by giving away an eBook in exchange for email addresses. Once a person opts in to your list, you have their permission to contact them and tell them about the products you have for sale. (Note: the gold is in the RELATIONSHIP with the PEOPLE on your list.)

3. Increase Your Visibility and Credibility. You will be viewed as an authority on the subjects you write about, provided you write informative and accurate eBooks. If you can persuade a more prominent author to co-write with you, you increase your credibility even more.

In return, your co-author will receive the benefits of increased productivity, more visibility, and more income.

4. Drive Traffic to Your Other Projects. Always include website addresses in your eBooks. There are many opportunities to tempt your readers to explore your sales sites.

WHAT TO WRITE ABOUT

Innovation is the creation of the new or the re-arranging of the old in a new way.

— *Michael Vance*

I can remember a time when there was no such thing as an eBook. I suspect that in the future all books will be eBooks. (I originally wrote this before the introduction of the Kindle, iPad and other electronic reading devices. I was right. They're not exclusively eBooks, but it's amazing how many books are available for immediate download and consumption now. Expect this trend to continue.)

Right now, the most successful eBooks are nonfiction. (This was true in 2006. It may not be true today, although it's probably true for self-published books.)

A look at the best-selling eBooks online reveals titles like: "How to ...," "The Ten Secrets of ...," and "Get Paid to ..."

There is a school of thought that says you should diligently research the search engines and current online directories to find out what people want, what eBooks are popular now, and then write your eBook targeting the identified market, regardless of your interest in or knowledge of that subject.

This strikes me as similar to trying to drive while looking in your rear view mirror. Although research is essential, this particular research only tells you what's behind you. It seems to come from a mind set of scarcity- as if you can only write one eBook! With the tools I'm about to give you, you can write an eBook a day (or several a day) if you want to.

The "next big thing" is going to come from someone who comes up with something new and different - why shouldn't it be you?

Pick a subject that interests you, and one that you already know something about. If you have experience working on cars, you might consider writing a book on basic automobile maintenance.

Target a specific market. This eBook is for people who are writing their first eBook, or are still in the "beginner" stage of their online journey. If I were writing for Literature Majors in Grad School, or previously published authors, I would write an entirely different book.

Using our example of a book on automobile maintenance, you could target housewives, teenage girls, senior citizens, or people who own vintage Fords. In my opinion, a book on that subject that would be valuable to all those groups would be too long and complex. You can write them all, but write them one at a time. Chicken Soup, anybody?

GET OTHERS TO WRITE YOUR EBOOK

To think creatively, we must be able to look afresh at what we normally take for granted.

— *George Kneller*

Another strategy for producing an eBook is to ask others to write it for you. Some of the most successful eBook promotions have featured eBooks with multiple authors. A good example is *The Myth of Passive Income*, http://mythofpassiveincome.com. I'll tell you about that in a minute.

Why would an author give you a chapter for your book?

Because you will encourage them to include their contact information and links to their web pages. That's why. The more copies of your book that you sell or give away, the more traffic they get to their sales sites. More traffic equals more sales.

(Note: you can also use existing articles or blog posts, with the author's permission. In some cases, you may want to write the chapter for them, and let them review and sign their name to it. If the author's name is well-known, or they're a noted expert in the field of your topic, it's worth doing a little extra work.)

Here's how I have used this technique.

At one of our weekly mastermind meetings, I cracked a joke about the myth of making passive income (http://mythofpassiveincome.com). I was whining because I had spent hours filling orders and answering customer service emails.

(Note: Let me tell you about it. This was early in my career, and I just had one computer. I was selling CDs online. I had to burn the CDs one at a time. Then, I had to print out the sticky labels and attach them one at a time. Then, I had to print out the covers, cut them to size, and insert them into the CD cases. Then, I had to put it all together. When you're selling a LOT of CDs, this is NOT passive income.)

This was the Internet age - I was supposed to be sitting on the beach smoking a Cuban cigar and drinking espresso while the money magically appeared in my bank account, wasn't I?

The reality, as most successful Internet Marketers will tell you if you catch them privately, is that most successful Internet Marketers work long hours to create passive income. Especially in the beginning of your career, passive income can be a myth. The idea is to "work once, get paid many times," but sometimes you have to work hard to put the machine in motion.

Dr. Joe Vitale laughed at my joke, and then decided it would make an interesting book. I suspect he also wanted to teach me a valuable lesson.

So, he and I contacted several of the top Internet Marketers and asked them to write a chapter about their passive income experiences. In a couple of weeks, we had 23 chapters, from some of the biggest names in the business.

I've made a LOT of passive income from a book about *The Myth of Passive Income*.

This technique will work for almost any subject. For example, if you wanted to write about running a successful online publishing company, you could email the owners of the most popular companies and ask them to contribute a chapter.

I suspect most of them would jump at the chance. Every copy of your eBook will be an advertisement for them.

When it came time to approach Joint Venture partners for the eBook, we approached the co-authors. They were happy to make money from the eBook. Of course, it would be interesting to their lists- since they're in it.

This generated a lot of sales (and it's still selling), but more importantly, each person they sent to our site had the opportunity to sign up for our list. This is a great technique for "creaming" another marketer's list. We were able to identify, and gain access to, the members of their list that were interested in our products.

This has led to some great relationships with our new subscribers, and subsequent sales of other products.

Get the idea?

USE INTERVIEWS TO WRITE AN EBOOK

What we call creative work, ought not to be called work at all, because it isn't. I imagine that Thomas Edison never did a day's work in his last fifty years.

— *Stephen B. Leacock*

A variation on having others write your book for you is to use interviews.

This is just a little more work, but there are a lot of benefits to this method. Remember that the interview can be conducted by phone, in person, by email- sometimes, the method you use to interview the expert can be a selling point. Be creative!

People who might not take the time to write a chapter are more likely to have a conversation with you, especially if you entice them with an ethical bribe - in this case, you can offer to include their contact and sales information in the chapter you create from the interview.

For example, suppose you wanted to write an eBook about the best way to buy a used car. You could arrange to talk with a broad range of used car sales-men. What are their tricks? What techniques do they use to get customers to buy? What should a customer ask? Look for? What should a customer be afraid of or concerned about?

Most salesmen will happily talk about their business, if you can convince them that it will attract more customers.

In this case, I'd ask them about the dirty tricks OTHER salesmen use.

If you're writing an eBook on a topic you're very familiar with, you can interview yourself. You're the expert!

Once you've got your interviews, you've converted your authoring problem to a typing problem. You can hire a transcription service to type it for you.

Writing your book from interviews has a hidden benefit- you now have an audio product to sell! You can use your interview tapes as the source material to create CDs or you can convert them to MP3s and sell them as digital products.

(Note: http://freeconferencecall.com is a free service that will allow you to do interviews over the phone and record them. I use a service called Go To Webinar, http://gotowebinar.com that allows me to not only record audio, but to record video of my computer screen, or the interview subject's screen. This is a powerful teaching tool, and makes for a valuable and easy to generate product.)

One example of an interview MP3 product is at http://ebookproblemsolver.com. I interviewed Dr. Joe Vitale on the subject of eBook production and marketing, converted the interview to MP3s, and put them online. After listening to that interview, you should be able to come up with a topic, write the eBook, get it online, and sell it. The whole production took less than four hours to create- and was a lot of fun.

Right now, the most popular eBooks (self-published) are the ones that explain how to do something: how to save money, how to make a web page, how to fix a car, how to satisfy your lover, how to bake a great cheesecake- even how to write an eBook!

You're looking for an expert to interview, but be creative about what constitutes an "expert."

Almost anybody can be an expert and a resource for a profitable eBook if you create the right questions.

Consider:

Real Estate Agents

Insurance Agents

Day Care Center worker/owner

Coffee Shop Employee

Internet Gurus

Secret Lives

Rags to Riches

High School Students

College Students

Retirees

Industry Survey

I'll bet you can come up with your own list. Each of those categories could be the impetus for multiple information products. Find the problems that people have in each one, and then find the expert with the solutions.

USE RESEARCH (SEARCH ENGINES AND SOCIAL NETWORKING SITES) TO WRITE YOUR EBOOK

The whole of science is nothing more than a refinement of everyday thinking.

— *Albert Einstein*

Another eBook-generating idea is actually as old as grad school, but the Internet makes it easy. It's called "research."

The word "research" brings back memories of confusion and frustration for me. Have they found the sadist that came up with the Dewey decimal system (Dewey?) and strung him up yet? I never did get it.

Google, on the other hand, I understand. Without having to resort to card files or surly librarians, I can type in the subject of my prospective eBook and hit "enter." This will return pages of links to information on my topic.

Remember the old saying: "If you copy from one source, it's plagiarism. If you copy from multiple sources, it's research." Remember to use your research as a source for your own creative content.

(Note: Expand your search to Twitter and Facebook, and whatever new Social Networking resources appear next. You can find experts, conversations, and resources quickly - and connect personally with them. By the way, there are experts all over the world, from all disciplines, sitting by the phone waiting for your call. You can find them at http://rtir.com.

USE LISTS TO WRITE YOUR EBOOK

Think left and think right and think low and think high.
Oh, the thinks you can think up if only you try!
— *Dr. Seuss*

Another popular eBook format is the "list." If you can think of 10, 21, 101 (or whatever) things that go together, you've got an eBook.

Come with your list. Then, expand on each item in that list. Each one of those is a chapter.

Here are a few ideas I came up with over a cup of coffee:

25 Tricks for Saving Money on Gasoline

101 eBook ideas

10 steps to the Perfect Cup of Coffee

17 Things You Must Know About Wine

99 Great Sandwich Ideas

19 Things to look for When You're Looking for a Computer

111 Dating Tips for the Shy Man

1001 Ways to Make Money with Your Computer

12 Secrets of Automobile Maintenance

25 Things Your Banker Will NOT Tell You

WHAT _____ CAN TEACH US ABOUT _____

Those who wish to sing, always find a song. Swedish Proverb

This chapter started as an article called "What Tom Sawyer Taught Me About Writing eBooks."

My friend, Bill Hibbler, wrote a popular series of articles called "What American Idol Can Teach Us About Marketing."

These are works of fiction, by the way. I don't know Tom Sawyer, personally. Use your imaginary source as a point of inspiration, and imagine what they would say.

Here are a few ideas:

What Sex Workers Can Teach Us About Politics
What Thomas Jefferson Can Teach Us About Love
What Captain Kangaroo Taught Me About Physics
What Jesse James Can Teach Us About Banking
William Shakespeare On Marketing
Gertrude Stein's Secrets of Communication
What Madonna Can Show Us About Marketing (a lot!)

BE AN ONLINE MARCO POLO

There is one thing stronger than all the armies in the world, and that is an idea whose time has come.

— *Victor Hugo*

In 1271, Marco Polo (at seventeen years of age), his father, and his uncle set off for Asia on the series of adventures that were later documented in Marco's book. They returned to Venice in 1295, 24 years later, with many riches and treasures. (from WikiPedia)

I've seen the future, and it's happening right now.

Do you spend much time reading tech blogs?

I'm waiting for my iPad, and not a bit patiently. Since I can't actually play with it yet, I started out reading blog posts about it. That led me to some other blog posts, and down the rabbit hole I scampered. It's kinda cool down here.

One thing I learned is that I'm guilty of tunnel vision. See if this sounds like you: "I work in, basically, two niches. I make products in those niches, and pretty much ignore all other opportunities."

Sound familiar? You frame yourself as an Internet marketer who makes Internet marketing products, and you're probably up-to-the-minute informed about what's going on in that niche. Me, too. I've seen the "latest technology" that the front-running marketers are using, and have adapted same to my business.

Friend, we don't know beans.

(My other niche is making inspirational and meditation audios, and I do most of my research on Pandora's New Age Instrumental channel.)

So, it took me a while to get my bearings in this exotic foreign country. Flash/Adobe vs iPad/Apple. Twitter is embedding meta-data (soon). Chatroulette, and its 17 year-old developer. Start ups. Venture capital funding. App developing across multiple platforms. Twitter blocking developers, Apple erecting a "Great Wall" around its app store, Facebook (of all things) becoming more open and developer friendly.

All of those data points represent a money-making opportunity for somebody. Is that somebody you?

Basically, I quickly realized that there are a LOT of ways to make money online. In fact, I kinda feel like Marco Polo, here. I've seen some other countries, and they're way cool. They do things differently, and it works.

So, first word of advice: get out more. Leave your niche behind for a day and talk a walk on the wild side. I think you'll find it inspirational.

Then, come home. Crawl out of the rabbit hole, and put what you've learned to work for you.

The first way to reframe your business with your new knowledge is to "go mainstream."

What I mean by "mainstream" is, if you're like me, you create products for a specific and finite market. In my case, I know what beginning Internet Marketers need to know because 1) I've been teaching them for years and 2) I've got an active forum and coaching program full of beginning Internet Marketers. We have coaching (un)Webinars every Tuesday night and I spend up to two hours answering questions.

The big question is, "who else could use this information?"

For example, I'm working on some video instruction products. Internet Marketers need to know how to make a good video. It turns out that, with minor tweaking, that product can also be of benefit to a LOT of other people besides Internet Marketers. I can serve my customers, and also serve the world at large. The "mainstream."

So - how can you reframe your products so that they can be of interest to more people? I think you'll be surprised. Everybody is online, and the same skills that, for example, you need to make a good marketing video are also valuable for making a video of a kid (or grandkid), or a vacation, or a big date, or...see what I mean?

While we're on the subject of making money, let me tell you about a coaching UnWebinar we had a couple of weeks ago.

Actually, let me tell you about a conversation I had with a very bright beginning Internet Marketer.

He's got one product. It's a continuity program. His plan is to rule the galaxy by getting 1,000 people signed up for his continuity program. To put it gently, he's got a long way to go.

He asked me what I thought he should do.

That's when I told him about the coaching UnWebinar.

A lot of my coaching students have the same problem. They worked, in some cases, months putting together their eBook or audio. Then they marketed it, and had some success.

That's the good news.

The less good news is that they aren't making enough money to live on from that one product.

The solution is obvious.

So, to drive my point home, I did something I would only do for my coaching students, whom I love. I logged onto my 1shoppingcart account and showed them where my money was coming from.

I've got about 100 active products, and about 75% of them are on 1shoppingcart. So, I brought up my sales for the last month. It wasn't an exceptional month, but it was several times what I used to make in a year. That wasn't the point.

The point was that each of those products contributed something to my income. Some - the new ones that I'm promoting heavily - contributed more. Others only contribute a few hundred dollars a month. It adds up. The income was a result of the cumulative effect of having all those websites promoting all those products.

Each time somebody buys a product, they're placed on a (confirmed opt-in) autoresponder list, and I use my autoresponder to help them learn about other products that they might enjoy. This is the old "product funnel" system, although I'm not as disciplined at it as some marketers. In my case, the funnel is very wide but not all that deep.

Traditionally, you'd want to start with a free product, upsell to a cheap product, and gradually upsell to a stunningly expensive product. I tend to sell horizontally - I have a lot of products in the low to mid price range. It works for me.

Either way will work for you.

I don't know any successful Internet Marketer who makes his living from just one product.

Back to the conversation - the objection raised was "it takes a long time to make a product."

My response was, "put your flip cam on a tripod and start talking. Can you say something in an hour that's worth $20? Sell five of those and you've made $100."

"Can you do it two hours in a row? Can you do it four times a day?"

If you've got something of value to say, you should be able to crank out products that fast.

If you want to make a product that will sell for more money, find an expert and interview them. Do it on the phone and record it, if they're too far away for a flip cam. You can do one of these a day, and still have time to play with your new iPad.

Just remember that the money is in solving problems. People will pay for solutions. If you don't know that solution, find somebody who does and stick a recording device in front of them.

Over time, you can build an inventory of products. Some will be home runs, and if you can predict which ones, you're smarter than I am. Most will be "base hits."

You can win the game with base hits. More importantly, you can't hit a home run unless you actually grab a bat with both hands and swing at a few pitches. I don't think you can actually strike out. I've never made a product that sold zero. You probably won't, either.

That's pretty much the talk I gave to my coaching students. Some of them got it right away. At first, I thought they were all playing with their iPads or watching TV... it got real quiet. When I asked them if they were still there, the general response was "shut up, I'm thinking!"

Some of them have actually made a few new products since then. My goal, as a coach, is to motivate them all. I'm working on it.

Now, I'm going back to cruising the tech blogs. If a 17 year old Russian kid can come up with a mult-million dollar idea, so can I. Eventually.

In the meantime, I'm making a few more products. They may be base hits, but you never know until you swing at the ball.

Keep swinging.

INTERNET MARKETING SUCCESS — ONE PLAY AT A TIME

An avalanche begins with a snowflake.

— Joseph Compton

I was sitting with my buddy Bruce Collie at his restaurant, Brewster's Pizza, talking about Internet Marketing. It was a couple of hours before the restaurant was to open for the day. Outside, it was kind of cold and nippy. Inside, it was warm. Pizza dough was rising and bell peppers were roasting, and a few of his and Holly's kids were playing and laughing.

Bruce is an amazing guy. Former San Francisco 49'er with two super bowl rings, very artistic architect and carpenter, world-class chef, parenting coach, inventor...and now, he wants to learn Internet Marketing.

As we talked, I realized that Bruce had a very common problem. Most of my coaching students have the same problem. He had so many great ideas that he was immobilized. He wanted to do so many things at once that he ended up doing nothing.

Sound familiar?

I thought a minute, and then said:

"The '89 49'ers could do just about anything that can be done on a football field, right?"

"Right," he said. He was in the starting line-up when Joe Montanna led them to their second Super Bowl victory, and has told me stories of the west-coast offense. At that time, they were the best football team in the world and they proved it.

"How many plays did you have in your playbook?" I asked.

He rolled his eyes towards the ceiling and shook his head. "Over 2,000."

"How many plays could you run at a time?" I asked. "It's first and ten from your 20, the first play of the game, and the ultimate goal is to win the game.

How many plays can you run on that particular first down?"

It took a few minutes, but he finally "got" it. The answer is "one."

It will take hundreds of plays to accomplish the goal of winning the game, but you can only run them one at a time. And, it's important to run the right play at the right time to maximize yardage. You need a winning strategy. You need to be open to your options and able to improvise when you need to. But, you have to run the plays one at a time.

Running a successful Internet Marketing business is the same way.

Sometimes, I get overwhelmed, too. There are just too many great opportunities. I want to do them all now. There are books to write, videos to film, audio products to make. We're launching Spanish and French versions of some of our products, and considering doing Dutch and German ones. There are always resources needed for my coaching program. And that's before I play my guitars, watch movies, hang out with Betsy and/or the kids, and smoke cigars with my friends.

The good news is that you CAN do it all. You just have to do it one thing at a time.

In the Portable Empire System, the focus is on solving problems and selling the solution. The core of your Internet marketing business should be:

- opt-in pages where you trade something of value in your niche for email addresses
- sales pages where you sell a product in your niche

Of course, you also need to build a relationship and maintain that relationship with your readers, create your autoresponder matrix, do social networking, develop JV relationships... but, I've found that the actual income results from building your list and selling products.

One opt-in page and one sales page represents one stream of income. It's highly unlikely that you'll be able to live the life of your dreams on the income from one product.

However, once you learn the Portable Empire system, you'll know lots of easy, simple ways to create products and get them online: public domain, master resale rights, video, audio, eBooks, teleseminars, webinars...

Again, the options can be overwhelming.

The key is to do the next right thing.

Put up the second opt-in page and sales page. There's your second passive income stream.

Then the next.

Then the next.

And, one day you look up and you've got a LOT of passive income streams flowing into your bank account.

It doesn't happen overnight. It happens over time - one step at a time.

Getting back to football- the game is won by a series of 4 and 5 yard plays. Every now and then, a running back will break a tackle and streak down the field for a touchdown. You can't plan for that to happen. However, if you don't run the play, you can guarantee that it won't happen.

Same thing with Internet Marketing. Success comes in increments. Get one site bringing in a few hundred dollars a month. Then another. Then another. Then, out of nowhere, you have a product that EVERYBODY wants and sales go off the charts. If you can predict which product is going to do that, you're better than I am.

I've had a few of those, and the feeling is great! But, I'm always surprised. Why did THIS product do six figures and THAT one struggle to do five? I can't predict it, and I can't duplicate it on command.

It doesn't matter. If you get enough streams of passive income flowing into your business, the surprise touchdowns will just be gravy. I have learned that your odds of having one of those surprises is directly related to the number of products you put out.

By the end of our conversation, Bruce had identified the ONE product he wanted to work on first. He's and Holly are going to do a short introductory video for their opt-in page and a longer one for their first product.

That's his first play.

What's yours?

An idea not coupled with action will never get any bigger than the brain cell it occupied.

— *Arnold Glascow*

Let's break out a bottle of virtual champagne and have a little online celebration. Let's go with Champagne Philipponnat Clos des Goisses 1999 Brut.

I hear it's pretty good. ;)

It was about six years ago that Bill Hibbler and I managed to sneak into Joe Vitale's "Spiritual Marketing Summit" in Austin. Joe had slipped us passes. Neither one of us could afford the $1,000 tickets.

It was held at the historic Driskill hotel, which was all aglitter. Home to cattle barons and politicians since 1886, it was an intimidating and luxurious setting for a seminar that was all about prosperity. Needless to say, we couldn't afford to stay there. We drove back to Wimberley each evening after the seminar, talking over what we'd learned that day.

Bill was already dabbling in Internet Marketing. I was still playing guitar "day to day and town to town." To me, it was all new and exciting. I've always been more or less unemployable. The yoke of a day job chafed immediately, and- for me- day jobs were mostly about paying the rent and killing time till the next tour.

At that seminar, I was introduced to a way to make a living- and live a lifestyle- that absolutely worked for me. My "weaknesses" suddenly were strengths. I like to sleep when I'm sleepy, travel when the wanderlust hits me, and will work like a fiend on projects that I find interesting. I've always said that "there's a word for people who do stuff just for money..." and, although there were times when I unloaded trucks in the Texas heat, or did some other mindless labor "just for money," I was honest with myself about why I was doing it and who I was while doing it.

I learned a couple of very important things at that seminar.

First, my assumption that Internet Marketers were somehow smarter than the rest of us was erroneous. I met several and they fell all over the spectrum. Some WERE brilliant. Some were not. None of them showed any tendency to walk on water or float through the air while doing advanced quadratic equations.

They were just folk, but folk who knew how to do Internet Marketing.

Second, I noticed that they tended to contradict each other. They all had a system for success. The systems were all different. In our conversations on the ride home, Bill and I decided that any of those systems would probably work- but that you had to choose one. Six years later, I'm still convinced that's right. That's why I tell my coaching clients to pick one guru (guru means teacher, BTW) for each skill. If you're going to study Michel Fortin's copywriting material, don't study John Carlton's or David Garfinkel's at the same time. They contradict each other. And they're all right. But, if you study more than one at a time you'll just get confused.

Finally, I discovered that I could create information products and sell them. I made some CDs of a few audio products I had created with Joe's guidance. One at a time.

Let me paint the picture for you- the audio files were on the hard drive of the only computer I owned. So, to create these products I had to burn CDs one at a time. Then, I opened the graphics program and printed out the CD labels, which had to be stuck to the CDs one at a time. Then I printed out the CD covers, which had to be cut out by hand and put in the cases one at a time. I spent the night before the seminar on my hands and knees in my office putting together what I thought was way too many CDs. At least, I thought, it will look good...

I sold all the CDs I brought the first day.

So, after driving home from the seminar, I spent hours putting together another batch of CDs. At the seminar the next day, I sold out again.

If you've got one of those CDs, congratulations. They're definitely collector's items.

Remember, this was at a time when I was playing bars around Texas for

$30-$50 a night, and selling my music CDs from the stage. On a good night, I might sell ten CDs. Most nights, one or two. In one weekend, I sold about 100 CDs, at more than twice what I charged for my music CDs. To me, at that time, it seemed like a lot of money made very easily.

I was hooked.

Creativity is allowing oneself to make mistakes. Art is knowing which ones to keep.
— *Scott Adams, The Dilbert Principle*

Product creation.

Want to learn how to create profitable products, interesting blog posts, web pages and articles quickly and easily?

Nothing to it. You just need to be prepared.

I take a digital camera everywhere I go. Every picture tells a story.

I use a lot of video. My YouTube channel has had hundreds of thousands of views.

I do a lot of audio interviews and products.

I hope you, the reader, find these things interesting. Welcome to my world.

However, let's think like Internet Marketers. The most important thing I teach is "build a relationship with your readers." Almost every time I send an email to my list, I get responses back from people who think I sent them that email personally.

And, I did.

However, I also sent it to tens of thousands of other people. Personally.

One good way to build that relationship is to let your readers into your world. When I go on vacation, or visit another marketer's seminar, or go to a party, I take along my tools.

When I'm out, and the opportunity presents itself, I'm just a few seconds away from capturing the moment.

Inside my black leather backpack, this is what you'll see. In addition to the billfold, 2 cell phones, and headphones, I carry a Flip Mino HD video camera, a Tascam DR1 MP3/Wave recorder, and a digital camera.

These are relatively inexpensive tools that are also good enough to make professional products and easy enough to use that I can concentrate on getting "the shot," and not have to worry about tech stuff. I've got much nicer video cams, but the Flip fits in my bag and takes video that is "good enough."

If you're in my coaching program, you've heard me say, "good enough is good enough." It's true. The "good enough" video or audio that you actually can put online beats the hell out of the "perfect" video or audio that you never seem to get. The Flip camp is perfect for getting "good enough" video.

That Tascam DR1, on the other hand, is overkill. For most applications, a $50 MP3 recorder from Office Depot would work just fine. The Tascam costs about $250, records WAV as well as high-quality MP3, and has two condenser microphones. It's a very nice piece of gear. Last week, I loaned it to my kiddo and his buddies who had a gig recording sound effects for a movie. It would take a LOT of gear to get a better sound than that little box can record.

If you've got the bucks, I recommend it. If not...well, good enough is good enough. The important thing is to have an audio recorder so that when the opportunity arises to interview somebody interesting, you're there- and you're ready.

Finally, there's the digital camera. At UnSeminar 7 somebody liberated my little Nikon. I liked that camera.

When I went to replace it, I had to make a decision. That Powershot SX20 is a little bigger than most pocket cams. It's smaller than it looks in that picture, but it's too bulky to actually put in a pocket. However, it's got some features that I find real attractive- really powerful optical zoom, for one thing- and it was just a smidgen more expensive than the pocket-cam I was looking at. Since I carry the bag anyway, I went for the mini-SLR. I'm very happy with the quality of the pics that camera takes. I'm very much a "point and shoot" photographer, and this camera never goes off the "automatic" setting. Good enough is good enough.

It's also more camera than you need- these days, even the cheapie digital cameras are better than the professional ones were a few years ago. On a scale of 1 to 10, you get 9 points just for having a camera when you need it. Nobody is going to critique your composition or color balance- we're just taking snapshots here.

The focus is on relationship building. Pics, audios, and videos can be put on your blog. They're great for getting testimonials and "perception" shots. You want as many shots of yourself with known marketers as you can get. Those help you build the perception that you want your readers to have.

Remember, we're marketers. This is branding.

However, your tools will pay for themselves quickly if you keep a "product developer's" mindset. Remember, we're in the business of solving problems. One of my most popular products is the "eBook Problem Solver."

That's just an audio of a conversation I had with Joe Vitale a few years ago about eBooks. How to make them, how to market them, what to write about, etc. I was still a relative noob at the time, and it was an interesting conversation. As a matter of fact, it's so interesting that you can build an entire eBook business with what you'll learn when you hear it.

What if I hadn't had my recording stuff there when the conversation took place? A lot of people would never have written their first eBook, and I would have missed out on a nice income opportunity.

Tools. Get 'em. Use 'em.

Creative minds have always been known to survive any kind of bad training.

— *Anna Freud*

In the last chapter we talked about audio, video and pics.

I like 'em. They're quick. They're a good way to build rapport with your readers, and to create products on the fly.

However, let's talk about those readers.

Recently, I put up a survey to find out what my readers want. Surprisingly, in this age of broadband access and video on demand, 49% of my readers want eBooks.

Actually, that's not all that surprising when you stop and think about it. When I really want to learn something, I much prefer the printed page. Recently, as part of "Project New Galt's Gulch," I've been learning PPC. I bought a few recommended courses- and one of them, Perry Marshall's *Definitive Guide to Google Adwords 2010*, was so good I decided to make that one of my two main resources. (The other one was Armand Morin's "Secret PPC" video series.)

Perry's eBook was almost 300 pages long. I printed it out. It's on my desk right now, along with a pile of notes I've taken as I work through it. I don't know about you, but when I decide to put my nose to the grindstone and really learn something, I want paper with words on it.

(Unfortunate sidenote. Just about the time I finished that course, Google changed their rules again and everything I had just learned was out of date. I don't do PPC at all, now.)

But then, I'm a reader. I'll spend all day in my office studying eBooks, and then unwind at night with a good book.

Every Internet Marketer I know who has had any kind of success at all BUYS Internet Marketing products. First of all, we're in a dynamic business. It changes daily. There's no way any of us can learn it all. So, I was tickled twisty-toed to be able to pay Armand and Perry a couple of hundred bucks to do my work for me. They did all the testing and research. They waded through all the BS and distilled the good stuff down into an easily digestible (well...300 pages...) chunk of information that I can use to make money.

Second, we need to know what our competition is doing. Sometimes, I buy an info-product, look at it, chuckle, and delete it. After a while, you learn who puts out good stuff and who's just rakin' the noobs for easy cash. But, sometimes, you can discover trends and strategies that you would never have heard about otherwise. Invest in yourself.

So- what's an eBook?

If you've been hanging out with me for any time at all, you know that I focus on solving problems. People will pay you to solve their problems. Find an interesting problem, package the solution, and then sell it.

I suspect that as eBook readers gain popularity - and who knows what the Apple tablet is going to do to the market - we'll need to learn different ways to deliver eBooks, but right now eBooks are delivered as PDF files.

So- to write an eBook, you find that solution and write it down. People (most people. the smart people.) don't value an eBook by weight or volume. They're looking for a solution to their problem.

You can use Microsoft Office to write the eBook, and then use a commercial PDF generator to create the PDF file- but, the easy solution is to download Open Office at http://openoffice.org. It's free.

Open Office is pretty much a Microsoft Office clone, and it includes a PDF generator. So, you can write your eBook with it, and then export it as a PDF.

That's all there is to it. No muss. No fuss.

Once you've exported your file as a PDF, you've got a file you can upload to a server and deliver to your customers. I use FileZilla to FTP files to my servers.

Once the file is online, you can create a download page, write your sales page, and start selling.

If you're curious about what to write about, how to actually write it, and how to answer the question "who'd read something I wrote?" you should check out the eBook Problem Solver. which is an audio course I did with Joe Vitale.

Of course, for detailed hands-on help with this and all subjects Internet Marketing, check out my Portable Empire Coaching program.

Final thought- the important thing is to do it. Writing and selling eBooks is the easiest and fastest way to start your Internet Marketing business. There's practically no barrier to entry- it doesn't cost anything at all to create eBooks. For less than $20 (for hosting), you can have your business up and running. Tonight.

NOW WHAT?

Easy, isn't it?

How many eBooks have you written so far? (remember, this is a book you DO!)

Keep at it. Use every new eBook as an opportunity to promote your previous eBooks.

AUDIO PRODUCTS

All riches have their origin in mind. Wealth is in ideas - not money.

— *Robert Collier*

Remember, you're in the business of selling solutions. The best way to deliver those solutions is the way you'll actually do it. Some people are writers. Some prefer to talk. Some like to make videos.

If you were stranded in the desert and dying of thirst, you wouldn't pay a lot of attention to the container your water came in. You'd pay whatever the price was for the solution to your problem, however it was delivered.

Let's look at a couple of other ways to deliver solutions.

I was a musician before I was an Internet Marketer, and I've had a recording studio of one kind or another most of my adult life.

When I made my first record (remember those?) in 1982, studio time was $125 an hour. When I closed down my commercial studio in 1995, I had hundreds of thousands of dollars worth of equipment in a 3,500 square foot space, and studio time was selling for $35 an hour. Now, I've got a $500 recording software program, and $250 outboard audio converter, and I've created six commercial CDs (released on ZYX records) and dozens of audio products in a small office. I record, basically, for free.

(I've also got about a dozen synthesizers and twenty-something guitars, in addition to various exotic stringed instruments and noise makers. I like 'em, but you don't need them to make Internet Marketing Products.)

For the purposes of making online audio products, the small Tascam MP3 recorder I carry in my backpack is more than sufficient. It's what I use for interviews.

If you'd like to put together your own home recording studio, you might want to start with a software program called Audacity. It's at http://patobryan.com/tools. It's free, and has some powerful editing tools. Add a $50 USB condenser microphone, and you're ready to create world-class audios. You can also load the audio from your MP3 recorder into Audacity, to take out the inevitable "ummms," wise-cracks and dead space.

Once you've recorded and edited your audio, you need to convert it to an MP3. Most audio software programs will export MP3s for you.

Then, put it online, create a download page, and sell it!

VIDEO PRODUCTS

The only limits are, as always, those of vision.
— James Broughton

When I wrote the first version of this book, most of the world was using dial-up modems to access the Internet. Streaming or delivering video just wasn't practical, unless you wanted to ship DVDs.

Today, we're streaming videos to our phones, iPads and laptops through wireless broadband, 3G (soon 4G), and video is every-where. And, it's gotten cheap to produce and deliver.

I got into video when I put on my first Seminar, UnSeminar 1. I bought a Canon XL1 and hired an operator for it. After the seminar, I had 30+ video tapes that needed to be edited. And no money. That made deciding who was going to do the editing pretty simple. I bought an inexpensive editing program and taught myself how to edit video. It's easy. You just take out the parts that you don't want, add titles, maybe some music, and you're done.

I produce and market a lot of video. Now, I've got several good video cameras, including high-def pro cams. I've got two Final Cut Pro editing suites. It was expensive, but it's paid for itself many times over.

However, you don't need to spend a lot of money to create video products. I use a $150 Flip HD for most of my video production. I use Adobe Premier Elements to edit most of my videos. I think I paid $75 for that. If you've got a Mac, it came with iMovie, which is a very capably editing program. If you're using a Windows computer, download the Windows Movie Maker software. It's free.

You can be in the video-product business for less than $200, and prices are dropping.

I carry my Flip Cam in my backpack, along with my digital camera and

MP3 recorder, so I never miss an opportunity to make a product, or snag content for a blog post, or add an interesting video to my YouTube channel. (search YouTube for Practical Metaphysics - I've got a LOT of video up there for you.)

Once you've edited your video, you need to render it in a format that customers can download and watch. Quicktime and Windows Media are good bets. Flash used to be a standard, but Apple is changing that by not supporting it on their products. You'll have to roll with the changes, here. This is going to change.

HTML5, whatever that is, appears to be the coming solution, but right now the video world is changing so fast that I'm not going to prescribe a video format.

Another type of video can be created with Camtasia (http://techsmith. com/camtasia.asp) or Go To Webinar (http://gotowebinar.com).

They both record audio and your computer's screen.

Camtasia is an excellent teaching solution, which makes it great for delivering solutions as products. If you want to show somebody how to do something online, or anything that can be done on or with a computer, I recommend Camtasia.

It's not inexpensive, but the uses you'll find for it make it a worthy investment. You can use it with Powerpoint to make video sales pages, for example.

Go To Webinar (http://go2webinar.com) is an online service, and it is not free. However, it's great for creating video content- especially if you're working with somebody else. I've done Webinars with experts all over the U.S. And Europe, and it works seamlessly. It records your voice, and anybody else's voice who is on the call (you get to choose whose mic is open.) I use a headset with a microphone that was designed for gaming when I do Webinars. The quality is just fine.

Once you finish your webinar, Go To Webinar, will automatically download the audio and video to your computer. Be sure to set your settings to "record using WMV." Once you have the downloaded recording, you can edit it in your video editing software.

BASIC INTERNET MARKETING STRATEGY

*The opportunities of man are limited only by his
imagination. But so few have imagination that there are
ten thousand fiddlers to one composer.*
                                    — Charles F. Kettering

One of my coaching students recently asked me about strategy. I hadn't really thought about that as something to teach.

After some reflection, I think she's right. There are some strategies that are universal enough that they're worth teaching. As you grow in your online business, you'll modify these and develop your own. Do what works for you.

Joint-Venture Strategy

*A Joint Venture (JV), as the term is used in Internet
Marketing, can be a loose agreement between a list-owner
and a product developer to work together marketing a
product or it can mean a more structured agreement where
two or more people work together on a project to develop
and market a product.*

Let's look at the first definition.

It's common for beginning Internet Marketers to start their careers by making products. Once the product is made, they have no one to sell it to.

The solution to this problem is to do a JV with somebody who has a list of people who are interested in that product.

Why would someone who has a large list be interested in marketing YOUR product?

Well, if you don't approach them properly, and have a winning strategy, they won't be.

The loop running through most people's minds, all the time, is Radio

WIIFM: "What's In It For Me?"

If your first contact with a list-owner consists of, "Hi, I'm ____. Would you hit your list for me?" You're going to experience epic failure immediately.

That's not how it works.

Joint Ventures work best when the relationship is already in place.

Here's how I teach my students to solve this problem.

First, identify your best Joint-Venture prospects. Google, Twitter, and Facebook are useful for this.

Then, build the relationship. ReTweet their tweets. Comment on their Facebook pages. Find their blogs and comment on those. After a while, they'll start to recognize you, and comment back. Then, send them an email. Tell them how much you enjoyed their latest product (you did buy it, didn't you?).

Then, and only then, mention that you've got a product that would be a good fit for their list. Only do this if your product is a good fit for their list.

The list owner is going to want to know some things about your product and your sales page(s). What is your conversion rate? What is your opt-in ratio?

Google Analytics is a free service (Google it) that will allow you to gather information about how many people are coming to your sales page, as well as where they're coming from and how they got there. Dividing the number of sales you make by the number of unique visitors to your website will give you your conversion rate. Dividing the number of people who sign up for your list by the number of people who visited your website will give you your opt-in ratio.

Now, remember Radio WIIFM? Your prospective Joint Venture partner will be curious about what's in it for them.

A strategy that has worked for me looks like this:

1. The list-owner sends an email to his readers offering a freebie that I've created (eBook, audio, video) in return for their email address. I use autoresponders - 1ShoppingCart (http://1shoppingcart.com) and/or Aweber (http://aweber.com) - to create the opt-in boxes. You can see one at http://absolutebeginnersguide.com.

The software automatically embeds a cookie in the customers browser. From that point on, if that customer buys a product, I'll know that the list-owner has earned a commission from that sale. That customer is his customer for the life of the agreement.

2. Once the customer signs up for their "freebie," I use the autoresponder software to automatically send them an email offering them an inexpensive product that is in the same niche as their freebie. You can load as many messages as you like into your autoresponder, and tell it how many days after the customer signs up to send each email. The list-owner makes a commission from each sale.

3. The customers who buy the inexpensive product are automatically taken off the "prospects" list and added to another list. They are also automatically sent emails offering them a more expensive product. When the customer buys, the list owner makes another commission.

4. Rinse and repeat. The customers who buy the more expensive product are then offered another product - possibly even more expensive - and moved from the second list to a third. This can be done automatically by the autoresponder software. As they continue to buy products, the list-owner continues to make commissions.

This is a compelling strategy and fairly easy to sell to a list owner. They send one email. They make money on those customers as a result of my effort and products.

Of course, those customers are now on my list, and I can market other products to them, too. Whether or not the original list owner makes commissions on all sales, or just the sales in the original series, is a subject of negotiation.

WHY YOUR BUSINESS HAS TO BE A DIALOG
OR: INTERNET MARKETING IS DEAD, LONG LIVE INTERNET MARKETING

The significant problems we face cannot be solved at the same level of thinking we were at when we created them.
- Albert Einstein

I host UnSeminars, which are widely acknowledged as being the most valuable seminars you can attend if you're interested in Internet Marketing.

Although I'm the host, I learn a lot at these gatherings. I bring in the best speakers in the business. I try to keep the attitude of "I know what I know, but I may not know what they know," and that keeps me attentive.

There's also a lot of down-time and hang-time at UnSeminars. I leave a lot of time for networking, and that's valuable.

However; the most important thing I learned, I learned from the other speakers and a few of the attendees who are veteran Internet Marketers: Internet Marketing is dead.

The original model for Internet Marketing (IM) was developed from age-old direct marketing techniques applied to a (at that time) new technology-email. It's a numbers game. The bigger your list, the more people you can email - and some percentage of those people will buy your product.

It's a monologue. The catch phrase for that kind of marketing is "buy or die." People either buy something or unsubscribe from the list. Or, more frequently, ignore the emails.

That's the old model, and it's deader than horseless carriages. Quaint. Picturesque. But, if your goal is to get somewhere, a Prius will do the job much better.

The whole online experience is changing.

Back in "the day," you'd put up an online brochure and that would be your web presence.

You'd put up a "sales page," and send traffic to it - and that would be your business.

Dead. Dead, I tell you. It's over. It's little feet are sticking straight up in the air and it's stiffer than a two by four.

Here's how dead it is. I talked to one long-time Internet Marketer whose sales are down by 90%. I talked to my speakers, and they told me that IM seminars are not selling out like they used to, and that back of the room sales are WAY down.

Yes, there are exceptions. The guys who have already made their millions- back in the olde days- have the bank-roll to move on. They can spend 7-8 figures a year on adwords. That's why your keywords are costing so much. You're competing with them. You're competing with WalMart and Amazon.com, now. The mainstream has discovered Internet Marketing, and to compete, you're going to have to be agile, creative, and smart.

So, should we all just pack it in? See if the local Starbucks is hiring?

That depends on you.

Can you change your marketing model? Can you adapt to the new paradigm?

What is this new paradigm?

Well, the central concept is that the days of the monologue are over. It doesn't matter how loudly you scream. It doesn't matter what colors or fonts you use for your headline. You can embed NLP hooks in your copy till the cows come home- and it doesn't matter. You're talking to yourself.

Your success will depend on how well you listen.

I shared my income numbers with some of the old-school marketers, and their jaws hit the floor. "In this economy, that's great!," they said.

Why is my business (and a few others who have caught on) thriving while other marketers, who have been doing this a lot longer than I have, are flopping like fish in the bottom of a bass boat?

My Portable Empire marketing system is based on service. And, I don't mean "do you want fries with that?" I mean, my model is based on actually helping people. Listening. Engaging in a dialogue or even (imagine this) get out of the way by providing an environment where your online followers actually engage with each other.

Every day, I get emails from other marketers. They're becoming shrill. "Buy my crap! Buy my new crap! Buy my new, improved, crap!"

It's over. Let it go. It doesn't work anymore.

Back in the dark mists of time, when "you've got mail" was a reason to smile and be amazed by the technology, that worked. Now, emails are something you wade through. They're a chore.

Where are people gathering? Twitter. Facebook. Forums.

But - first, a warning. If you just move your current model to Twitter and Facebook, you're going to fail magnificently. Some people are actually automating their spam on Twitter. They're the first to get blocked. Nobody is interested in your spam. Quit doing it.

Where these tools get powerful is when you listen.

What problems are people having? Where does it hurt? What are they really interested in?

Listen. They'll tell you.

The Portable Empire system is based on finding those golden problems, solving them, and selling the solutions. It's also based on building a relationship with the people on your lists.

At UnSeminar7, I was having breakfast with Trapper, Jennifer, Geoff, and Chuck - I think - the weekend is a blur - and we were talking about the Un-Seminar. I asked them, "what is the most valuable part for you?"

The answer didn't surprise me: "The relationships."

There was a great deal of hugging and smiling going on. People discovered what they had in common, and what they could help each other with. Joint-ventures were formed. Co-writers found each other. People with techie chops teamed up with creative types and formed alliances.

These are my customers!

Every attendee left with valuable new contacts, information, and aspirations - and their relationships with each other was the most valuable piece of the puzzle.

Yes, the speakers gave great information. Yes, the attendees were inspired. But, the most valuable part was the relationships that were forged. At UnSeminars, the speakers hang out with the attendees. We ate, talked, drank and smoked cigars until the early morning hours. The attendees pulled out their flip-cams and recorded interviews. They got to know the speakers, and, in some cases, the speakers got so excited about their ideas and enthusiasm that they agreed to work with the attendees.

This is the same model I use in my Portable Empire Coaching Program, and at my free MilagroWorld forum. People helping people. In the coaching program, we've been doing class projects. People help people and they all work together. Some of my students have grown their lists to several hundred people, already. And they're building relationships with their readers. Some of them have made hundreds of dollars online using the Portable Empire system.

More interestingly, out of these "artificial" partnerships, some very real business alliances have been formed. By helping their customers and helping each other, they're winning. And, it's happening fast.

I encourage my Coaching students to bring products to UnSeminars. At UnSeminar7, some of my attendees outsold some of the speakers.

That, my friends, is the future.

It's happening now.

SOCIAL NETWORKING: THE BUZZ FOR YOUR BIZ!

The universe is full of magical things patiently waiting for our wits to grow sharper.

— *Eden Phillpotts*

Martha Giffen

Once your business has a website up and running, you will want to participate in social networking.

There's nothing new about business networking. Many small business owners are members of their local Chamber of Commerce, Rotary, Lions Club, BNI, etc. These are organizations that business people meet others for the purpose of gaining new clients and gaining referrals.

Social media networking is the same thing. The connections are just not "in person." They are just as powerful, nonetheless.

I happen to be of the opinion that there's a right way and a wrong way to approach social media. By right, I mean, a way to increase your clients without constantly shouting to the world who you are and what your product is. By wrong, I mean, just using social media for advertising. If you are happy having a billboard ad and nothing more to advertise your business, then by all means, go do that. If you are interested in connecting with current, past, and future clients, then this is for you.

I am going to state what you already know: People buy from people they know, like, and trust.

Ask any small business owner and they will agree. The most successful and prosperous businesses are relational.

Think about it. Whether you are the first person your customer sees when they walk into your storefront or you are the door-to-door salesman, people buy from YOU! Period.

Soooooo, let's talk about how to get people to warm up to you on the world wide web, come into your store, and buy your goods!

TWITTER

Everybody's heard of it but many just don't "get it." Think of Twitter this way: There are many people in a huge room, some talking all at once, and some just standing in the corner quietly observing. You walk in. Most likely, you will look around, possibly see someone you know, or someone interesting that you don't know and you will strike up a conversation. Right? That's the beginning of networking. You are probably not mentioning your business at that point. You are just offering friendly conversation. As the conversation progresses, you mention your business and either give them a card, tell them you'll call, whatever. The point is, it's relaxed. You aren't walking into the room carrying a neon sign telling the whole room "buy my stuff, buy my stuff." Right?

The same rules apply to twitter. You will begin to engage in short conversations, people will start to know and like you and you eventually mention your business. Even promote your business.

Now, when you walk into the room at a live business networking event, usually people are wearing nametags. The great thing about twitter is that your "nametag" or who you are is listed for everybody to see, right underneath your picture. See? No neon sign necessary! And, you can even create a twitter background with your company logo and make that as personal as you like!

Think of your twitter background and profile as your "ad" for your biz. The "relational" part comes in the "tweeting."

The Basics

First, if you have not done it yet, go sign up at http://twitter.com

It's free and will only take a couple of minutes.

Two words of advice here: Always use your real name as your user name, especially if you are trying to brand yourself. And, upload a picture to be used as your avatar. Twitter is social. Many will not communicate with you if you are hiding behind the twitter bird!

The Lingo...

Just like everything else, Twitter has it's own lingo. Here's the main verbiage:

Tweet – The actual words you type on your status. Tweeting is a synonym for talking.

Retweet – Repeating something someone else tweeted.

It also consists of the use of abbreviations.

Here are a few:

@ before each person's name is used when communicating on twitter. It's public.

D before a person's name is used for private conversation. It's a direct message just between two people. Not public. You can only send direct messages to people who follow you.

RT means you are "retweeting," which is simply repeating something someone else has already tweeted or "said." This is done when someone has made a comment you find interesting or is promoting something you like.

How to "tweet"

Basically, twitter is a place where you have 140 characters to say whatever you want. The words you put out there are your "tweets."

Here are some basics to remember:

Be engaging.

Even though you may eventually use some canned promotional tweets, you need to be there "for real" for the most part.

"Retweet" something someone else has said that you think is clever, is similar to who you are, or is relevant to your list. Retweet from one of your customers. Look busy! Say "I'm headed out to meet with a new client, or. . .Lunch today at the best restaurant in our area". . . or just give a shout out to one of your customers. They love it and will bring you business!

The people who are the most successful on twitter are conversational. If someone tweets a comment to you, tweet something back. That's how the whole thing gets started. Talk to your customers!

If you are writing the blog and have great info, put that link in your tweet.

Something like "I love what I do" and include your website link.

"I'll be at ___ for lunch, if you are around, come up and say Hi"

"Anyone else headed to the Hoover Rotary today?"

Let them know that you are doing business, that you are busy, and you love what you do, adore your customers and would love referrals. You don't have to use any of those exact words. Just communicate. They'll get the message.

Whatever you offer that is unique to your niche, push THAT. Always. If you have great interviews on your site, say it. If you always follow back your twitter followers, say it. Use testimonials in your tweets. For example: "Just left ___. Been doing business for years. Such a great guy!" and give link to their business.

Be helpful. Tweet good content. If your niche is weight loss, tweet out good weight loss tips. People will start to expect that from you and will welcome what you have to say. They will also retweet to their followers, which could, in turn, lead to more followers (and possible future clients!) for you.

A word about your followers...

Treat them with respect. There is a reason they are following you. You have what they want, you are interesting, or they perceive YOU as a potential customer.

Your followers are numbered. That makes the math easy. It also can play a nice little head game on you. There are two strands of thought on this. One is you want to have "quality" followers. Followers that are only there because they know and love you. The other thought is the higher your numbers, the better. Those folks subscribe to the belief that sales is simply a numbers game and the more numbers, the more chances of making an online sale.

I say both are right. It depends on your market. If your market is the whole online world, then go for the numbers and let the chips fall where they may.

If you are after a targeted market, for example, your local market or a specific niche, my suggestion is to go for quality, and build your numbers from there. Also look at who is following your competition. You should try to get them to follow you too!

All in all, my philosophy is to start your list with a small targeted market and build the numbers from there. You will slowly build up a customer base with others on the peripheral scattered in. It's a nice mix.

For example, I have close alliances with many people who have on-line businesses whose products I don't actually need or use. However, I might retweet something they are saying about their product because I know, like and trust them. And also, who knows? There may be someone following me who NEEDS that product and I have just done them a service!

What is the best way to pick up followers? Tweet great content! Give little known facts, links to a great blog post, links about your niche, or links to articles about your niche. People are looking for great content. Give it to them! Turn yourself into the twitter expert about that particular niche. Engage in conversations with others who are interested in the same topics. Never forget, on your website or in social networking, ultimately content is king!

Promoting Other People

If all of your conversations are about you, your website or your product, you won't be looking at adding many followers.

What about promoting other people? This is a great way to increase your followers and also create goodwill among other business people.

When you recommend their websites or products, you are telling people "These are my favorites. I like what they are doing. I like their products and you will too!" This does two things for you. After that promotional tweet for someone else, you have endorsed what they are doing and they take note of it and probably at some later date, they will reciprocate. Also, it creates the image of being helpful to your clients and not just trying to push your products on them.

Isn't it always great when someone else says your product is fantastic? Not only does it have the possibility of producing a random sale for you but it increases your brand presence because now, all of his followers have seen the recommendation.

See where this is headed? Into the great big twitterverse of people! Possible customers you would have never encountered. Just because someone else promoted your product!

It's a big world out there! Does it feel like it just got bigger?

A word of warning: Never tweet a link that you haven't actually read! Sincerity is key!

140 Characters Not Enough?

Yes, 140 character is not very many. That's the beauty of Twitter. Nobody has a chance to go on and on about ANYTHING!

There IS a way to shorten urls or links that you are tweeting out. Here are three places you can go to shorten the link:

http://is.gd/

http://bit.ly/

http://tinyurl.com

I use all three and they are all great. You can decide which one shortens enough for you!

Automation and tools

Many business people have started automating their tweets. I don't really like it and don't often do it. Here's why: I am an advocate of relational selling. I can't be relational if there are canned tweets out there. However, having said that, I have been known to use a few on occasion, during my sleeping hours!

Twitter is a constant stream of people who are "in the moment." Chances are, they are going to see your tweet if they happen to be on twitter at the same time. Well, that's true, but due to Twitter Lists and some other clever applications, you can overcome this obstacle.

As you progress with your social networking, you will eventually want to add a few tools. There are many tools created for twitter that you can check out and see if they are for you.

Here are a few and what they do:

Tweetdeck – A great tool for keeping up with your messages. You won't miss any! This tool is focused on who is saying what about you! You can also tweet from there.

Tweetchat – A tool used to watch a #hashtag stream. Just enter the hashtag and the stream comes up. Has the capability of storing tweets to send out later. You can also tweet from there too.

Socialtoo – Sends stats of who has followed and unfollowed you every day. Also, has the capability to connect your twitter account with your Facebook account.

TwitterGrader – Let's you know your twitter rank. This is interesting information that you can tweet out.

MrTweet – Can help you find followers.

Twello – Called the "Twitter Yellow Pages" for a reason. It's free and will connect you with more people in your niche. A great place to register yourself! Remember, you want to be found too! You also have the capability of sending tweets from there.

Hootsuite – A place where you can manage all your social networking in one place. Can tweet from there and see multiple streams. It also has the capability of storing tweets to tweet later.

Twitpic – an application that lets you share photos on twitter.

Twitterholic – A site where you can get stats on yourself and other twitterers. Fun information!

#Hashtags

You will notice in some tweets, there are words with the # sign in front. That is called the hashtag. Using the hashtag creates a quick way to identify with a list of people who are all tweeting about the same subject. It's also a perfect way to add followers that are tweeting about your niche.

For example, If you type the hashtag #LOA, you will find a group of people tweeting about things relative to the Law of Attraction. Using the hashtag #golf would connect you with anyone tweeting something about golf.

You can even start your own hashtag. Just tweet something using a hashtag and see if it will catch on!

Trending Topics

On the right sidebar, you will see the Top 10 Trending Topics. If you click on "change," you can set it to a location. I always use "WorldWide" but you can set it for a certain country or even certain cities. It's another way to keep your pulse on what people are talking about at any given time. If one of the topics interests you, click on it and you will be taken to the twitter stream of people talking about that particular topic. Always remember, if any of those topics fit in your niche, check out that stream and follow anyone who is of interest to you!

And, be sure to participate in the conversation if it is relevant to your niche!

Twitter Lists

One way Twitter has become easier to stay connected with your core groups is by using the Twitter Lists. You will see it on the right hand side of the twitter page. You can create your own lists to make your life a little easier. And, you should be happy when other twitterers add you to their list. That way, you have a little more information about why they are following you in the first place!

When you create your lists, give them clever names. Don't title them "future clients" or "prospects". No, no, no! Would you want to be on a list with that label? Give them names like "cool peeps," "just met", or, like one I'm on, "B'ham peeps." That person is identifying my town, Birmingham.

The Power of Twitter

The great thing about twitter? You gain access to people that you would never have otherwise. In my case, I have found people to interview, chatted with famous authors, gotten technology help, and even an online mentor!

Use twitter wisely and you'll be watching your business grow.

FACEBOOK

Another social networking site is Facebook. It took a while for this one to catch on, but once it did, holy cow! Everybody and their brother is on there! Facebook is great for your online business. You have a lot of freedom to advertise and many ways for your "friends" to get to know you.

The basics

To set up your account on Facebook, simply go to http://Facebook.com and sign up for an account. Again, there will be plenty of fields for you to fill in the blanks. There are a lot of categories. Just answer the ones you want people to see. It's my opinion that the more you put out there, the more "humanized" you are and that is good for your business. It's your personal preference.

Your profile will be public. This is the place to let people know who you are and what you are doing. Put the link to your website for everyone to see! There is also a field for a short bio. Be sure you make a short statement that says exactly who you are and what you are doing. "I'm a Mom of three boys" is somewhat interesting, but "I help new online entrepreneurs achieve success with Internet marketing" is more specific. By the way, both of those descriptions describe me, but guess which one brings in clients?

And, I can't say this one loud enough – be sure and put your picture on your profile! People want to do business with you. Let them see who you are!

When looking at the Facebook page, you will see there is a "home" and "profile" page. On the home page, you will see the real-time stream of other people's status updates. You will also see on the upper right hand side the "requests" heading. You click on these to find out any friend request, fan page request, etc. On the profile page, you will see your profile, your status updates, your FB "friends," basically all things you!

Facebook also has FB message capability. This is e-mail to your account from other FB members.

There is also live chat capability. You will see at the bottom of the right hand side a little "chat" bar. You can optimize this and see which one of your friends is logged on. You can instant message them if you want to talk in "real time."

Warning on this feature: Do not abuse it! If you want to talk to family members and close friends, fine. Do not IM "friends" that are possible clients or mentors that you don't actually know unless you have a really good reason. It's intrusive. It's also a great way to get yourself "unfriended!"

How to use

Facebook is all about "friends." Who can be your friend on Facebook? Any one you approve. When you make a friend request, nothing happens until the other person accepts. Once that happens, you both have access to one another. It's that simple.

Always remember that social networking for your online business is about branding. Facebook is no different. There are many ways to make your presence known on Facebook.

First, your status update. It is that little line where you say something about what's going on in your life. At the very least, you should update it every morning. Yes, every day. You make it part of your daily marketing routine. It will become second nature in no time! Also, during the day, if possible, update. It's a great way for people to start to know you. Now, I'm not saying tell your deep, dark secrets on Facebook, but if you are meeting with a client, say it. (You can omit their name) If you are finishing a chapter in your book, say it. Why? You need to look like the busy entrepreneur that you are. Let the world know what's going on with you.

Busy businesses get more business. Idle ones watch their silent phones.

Here's a great example from the real estate niche. A certain Realtor is constantly updating her status to say, "I'm showing houses today," or "I'm heading out to a closing," or "I just listed a beautiful property in such-and-such subdivision." In between those updates, she is saying things like "I just finished eating at Local Joe's Restaurant, the food was great," or "Warren Buffet says the housing market is coming back to life in this article (she gives the link)." Now, tell me, when you get ready to pick a Realtor, does she look like one who is WORK-ING? You bet! And, that's the one people will call.

Same principle applies with your online business. Let your "friends" know you are busy. It will result in business AND referral business. Again, it's all about branding. Let your friends know you are churning it out and that you are glad to help them too.

If you have a promotion going on, say it. Give the link to it. If you are interviewing someone, put it out there. Did you just write a great blog post? Put that in your status and include the link! If you have a new product, or are just working on a product, put that in your status. Again, you want people to know that you are the expert or the "to-go-to" person in your niche.

Communicating with Others. . . .

As you begin to add friends to Facebook, you will be looking at their profiles also. You have the ability to write on their "wall." This is the stream on their profile where their status shows up. If you have a comment that adds to a discussion, fine. Otherwise, you don't want to write on walls too often. Just enough to let people know you are approachable and not become annoying.

Another caution: Do NOT write any type of ad for your business on someone else's wall. I know it's tempting to say, "Go look at my website" and add the link, but don't do it. Use the golden rule here!

Profile Applications

There are a number of applications (Apps) included with your profile. You will see them as tabs at the top of your profile page. These are: Video, Photos, Events, Groups, Notes, Posted Items, Gifts. These are different ways of enhancing your "friends" exposure to you when they visit your profile page.

Here are a few tips regarding these apps:

Video: You have the capability to upload videos. They must be under 300 MB and less than 20 minutes long. You can upload from your phone or web cam. It also have photo tagging capability.

Photos: To upload photos, click on "Create a Photo Album." You can also tag photos by clicking on the picture of the person. A box will come up for you to insert that person's name. If they are one of your friends on FB, it will appear on their wall as well.

Links: Any time you share a link on your status, it will be recorded here.

Fan Page

After you have set up your account, you will want to set up a Fan Page. This was a hard one for me at first. Who wants to be my fan? Well, you will be surprised. You send the invitation to everyone who is your friend on FB and watch them line up to be your fan. The great thing about the fan page is the capability of sending a group message to people who are genuinely interested in your business. You can send Facebook e-mails to them and such. It's just another great way to promote yourself.

A Little More Advanced...Facebook Apps

You can go to the left hand column and see "Applications." When you click on there, you will find lots and lots of apps for FB. Here are a few you might like for your online business:

Networked Blogs – A great application if you are writing blogs. You enter your blog link, it shows up on your profile page, and you can invite people to follow it. It's a great way to pick up more readers to your blog.

Twitter Badges – Links your twitter account to your FB account so you don't have to update both.

My LinkedIn Profile – Puts a LinkedIn Badge on your FB profile. Clicking the badge will take people to your LinkedIn Profile.

Facebook Connect – This will connect your website to Facebook

WARNING: Do not use the FriendFeed app because this posts all links and comments to all of your friends' walls. It is annoying to them! Trust me.

Another place to look for great apps is http://www.facebook.com/apps/directory.php

LINKEDIN

LinkedIn is a social networking site specifically designed for business owners or upper level managers within large companies. LinkedIn is where you show the face of your business. It is totally devoted to helping entrepreneurs and other business professionals connect.

If you haven't already, go to LinkedIn.com and sign up for an account. It's free.

Fill out your profile. Again, be sure and upload a profile picture!

Search for others in your field or niche.

A great way to turn yourself into an "expert" is to answer questions on LinkedIn "Questions and Answers" section. This is a great place to toot your horn without actually doing it yourself!

Always ask your clients for a LinkedIn recommendation and also, be wiling to recommend others you have worked with.

Even though LinkedIn is considered a social network, it is more of a business network. It is harder to connect with people you don't know, so my suggestion is build your network with people you already DO know and go outward from there.

Conclusion

Social networking is a way to have an ongoing conversation. With conversation, you build loyalty. You seem approachable. Your future customers will begin to know, like, and trust you.

Don't get too serious with it. Have fun. Be social. It's all about the networking!

Of course, I wouldn't be much of a social networking diva if I didn't include my own social links! You can find me at:

http://faceBook.com/marthagiffen

http://twitter.com/marthagiffen

http://linkedin.com/marthagiffen

Also, remember, through social networking, you just might meet a marketing guru that wants to include you in their new book!

Happy networking!

HOW TO WRITE A WRITE A SALES LETTER THAT PUTS A .357 MAGNUM TO YOUR PROSPECT'S HEAD... DEMANDS HE READS EVERY SINGLE WORD... AND FORCES HIM TO HAND OVER HIS HARD EARNED CASH!

Flaming enthusiasm, backed up by horse sense and persistence, is the quality that most frequently makes for success.

— *Dale Carnegie*

Colin Joss

If you want your sales letter read like a 14-year old boy reads his first Playboy then you'll want to read every word in this chapter.

Why? Because I'm about to expose a stunningly simple 4-step formula for writing a kick-ass sales letter known to only a handful of million-dollar copywriters.

It doesn't matter if you're giving away a freebie to build your list or you're selling the latest get-rich-quick course... if you follow this step-by-step system you'll write the best damn sales letter you possibly can.

But maybe you're wondering...

Who The Hell Is This Guy?

My name is Colin Joss ... and when it comes to writing copy I've been through the wars... and I've got the scars to prove it. Back in 2005 I discovered people were making money online. Not just a few dollars selling junk on eBay but thousands of dollars every month! Enough money to give up their day jobs, work from home, and spend more time with their families. For a guy who was travelling 2 hours each way to a dull office job, making money online sounded pretty damn good. I jumped in feet first into the Internet marketing world and bought every eBook, video, and course I could get my hands on. I spent hours every single day learning all the weird and wonderful jargon... autoresponders, squeeze pages, affiliates, domains, back links, HTML, and a whole lot more. Studying all that technical mumbo jumbo killed a lot of time. Eventually I knuckled down and started creating my first product. It was hard work but I got through it... slowly. But I ran slap-bang into a brick wall! I had to write copy to sell the damn thing! To be honest, writing copy scared the hell out of me. If I wrote crappy copy it would kill my sales and kill my dreams of making money online. But what could I do? I'd no other choice. I wrote the copy slowly. Painfully. Word by word. Sentence by sentence. It took weeks. But finally I had my first sales letter finished. I gritted my teeth and put it online. I sat at my beat-up kitchen table and waited for the sales to roll in. And they did! Over $1,000 in the first day. Over $5,000 in the first week. And over $30,000 in the first year!

But it all went down hill after that...

I Murdered My Marketing Career With Sales Copy That Sucked! My next three product launches crashed and burned. Each one worse than the last. Dreams of working from home as a full-time marketer twisted into thoughts of failure and frustration. I couldn't understand it. Why had my first product made a bundle and the others barely raked in a few hundred dollars? I scratched my head for a few weeks but I came up blank. I knew it had to be something to do with the sales copy. I'd got a truckload of people hitting my websites but hardly anyone bought a damn thing. So I paid John Carlton – the world's #1 copywriter – close to $1,000 to review one of my sales letters. John's a take-no-prisoners kind of guy. His response was pretty blunt. "Your copy sucks!" John went on to rip me a new asshole and tear my copy to shreds. "You lucked out with that first sales letter. You hit a hot niche at the right time. That's all. You can't write copy for shit!" That pissed me off! I'm a stubborn S.O.B. The moment I heard Carlton tell me "You can't write copy for shit!" I was hell-bent to prove him wrong! I shut down my struggling Internet marketing biz. I was going to become a kick-ass copywriter ... even if it killed me. I buried myself in the copywriting classics and the new stuff. I blew a wad off cash with a famous writer's institute. But I still didn't get it – copywriting was still a mystery. I beat my head bloody for another year before I made a breakthrough.

John Carlton – the same guy who'd torn me apart – offered to teach me his copywriting system! The same system he'd used for over 25 years to create sales letters that created fortunes for the biggest publishers in the world ... as well as countless entrepreneurs. I was stuck between a rock and a hard place! Part of me wanted to do it all by myself. To tell Carlton to go to hell...I'd figure it out on my own. (I told you I was stubborn as a mule.) But then I realized I'd be dumber than box of hammers not to grab John's offer with both hands. I signed up and...

I Almost Emptied My Bank Account To Peer Inside John Carlton's Bag Of Tricks! I spent close to $50,000 and over 8 months learning Carlton's copywriting secrets. But enough about me.

It's time you grabbed a yellow legal pad and a pencil. You've got some hard work to do...and some hard thinking.

Before you start cranking out copy you've got to ask yourself one tough question.

Who's The Guy That's Going To Buy?

I've got some bad news for you. The whole world isn't sitting on the edge of their seats waiting to buy your new product. To be brutally honest, 99.9% of people don't give a damn about you or your product and never will.

It's up to you to target the 0.1% that has a burning need for your product. The people who must have it... can't live without it. How do you do that?

You imagine you're a private eye hired to stalk your prospect and ferret out every dirty little secret he's hiding. You need to know your prospect better than his own mother. In fact, you need to discover something about your prospect that would shock... SHOCK... his own mother!

In marketing techno-babble, this breaks down into
Demographics
Geographics
Psychographics and
Technographics.

You've heard of demographics, haven't you? It's your prospects age. Are they male or female? Employed? Blue collar or white collar?

Geographics is pretty obvious too. Where they live...county, state, city. Even down to the neighborhood and street if it helps.

But what about psychographics and technographics? Psychographics is all about your prospects life. What are their interests? Hobbies? What associations do they belong to? It covers their culture. Did their ancestors arrive on the Mayflower and they still have a puritanical streak? Or maybe they're first generation Russian immigrants? You've got to know this stuff.

And most importantly you need to know their buying history. Do they hand over their credit card and buy the first thing they see? Or do they research every last detail before they reluctantly hand over their hard earned cash?

Finally, there's technographics. Does your prospect own a PC? Or does he insist on pounding away on a beat-up typewriter? Does he surf the web? Every day? Every week? Does he buy stuff on line? If so, what and where?

Phew! That's a lot to think about before you even start cranking out your copy, isn't it? But it's exactly what you must do. It's...

The Reason Most Marketers Crash And Burn!

They don't knuckle down and do the hard work to learn about their prospect. Marketers that fail miserably use a scattergun approach, trying to hit as many people as possible and hoping that some of them buy.

And when the marketing dies a death they sit back and scratch their heads and wonder why! But not you. Not now you know how to lock your prospect in your sights.

But before you pull the trigger you need to make the bullet – your sales letter – that you'll fire at your prospect. And that's where you need...

The 4-Step System for Writing Killer Copy

Think you can't write a sales letter? Think again. If you can sit on a bar stool and shoot the breeze with a complete stranger you can write a sales letter.

Picture this... You're sitting in an airport bar heading home after a long trip. You're nursing a cold beer and watching the game on the TV above the bar.

There's a guy sitting next to you wearing a crumpled suit and a worn out expression. He looks like you feel.

He's moaning to the bartender about his airsickness.

You turn to him, clap him on the shoulder and say "Hey buddy I know how you feel. I tried everything. Dramamine. Benadryl. But they just knocked me out and I woke up feeling like crap."

Then I tried those wrist bands but they were no damn good. Heck, I even tried acupuncture but it didn't work."

As you rattle off all the stuff you've tried, he starts smiling and nodding his head. "Yeah, me too."

But at last I found one thing that did work. Now I just kick back and enjoy the flight."

He leans forward eagerly. "What is it? What did you find?"

It's a strange herbal tea made from a small orchid only found in the low reaches of the Orinocho river. The local tribe make it and I import it from them."

What does it do?"

The natural plant extracts soothe the part of the brain that causes airsickness so you can sit back and relax even if the flight's as bumpy as the wildest roller coaster."

And it doesn't make you drowsy. In fact, you get to your destination feeling refreshed and buzzing with energy."

If you travel a lot you'll know how bad turbulence can be. And if you suffer with airsickness it's a thousand times worse. But with this herbal tea you'll never suffer again."

All you do is drink the tea before you go on the flight. It's as simple as that!"

Sounds good," he says. "But I'm not sure it'll work for me. I've tried a lot of stuff."

Aren't you sick and tired of dreading every flight? Isn't it embarrassing as hell sitting next to a hot girl and spending half the flight puking into a paper bag? With this herbal tea you'll never suffer again. You'll sit back and enjoy the flight. You'll watch the movies and chat with the hot girl. Heck, you might even feel like eating the airplane food!"

You reach into your pocket and pull out a teabag along with your business card. "Here's a sample. If it doesn't do exactly what I said it does then you owe me nothing. But when it stops your airsickness, and you arrive home feeling refreshed and with more energy, then call me on 247-555-0123, give me your address and credit card details, and I'll send you a whole box for only $19.97."

What have you got to lose? Keep on suffering with airsickness or try this out for free and have a great flight?"

He grabs the teabag and your card. He turns to the bartender and asks for a cup of hot water.

Get the picture? Writing a sales letter is as simple as having a conversation.

Here's a breakdown of how it works.

Step 1 - Here's Who I Am

In this first step of writing killer copy you introduce yourself and tell your story.

Why? To show empathy and build your credibility.

Who are you mostly likely to buy from? The sharp dressed shyster who walks up to you and simply says 'Buy my stuff!" Or the guy who looks like he's slept in his clothes but sympathizes with your problem because he's gone through the same thing too.

Look back at the scene about the man suffering with airsickness. In the scenario, you showed you were just like him. You'd tried all the pills and potions he'd tried. And just like him they hadn't worked.

He's sitting there nodding thinking 'At last! Someone else who goes through hell every time they catch a flight. Someone who understands me!'

Instead of being a stranger trying to selling him something, you've become a friend sympathizing with his problems and letting him know he's not alone.

And then you tell him you discovered a solution to his problem. You've got an answer to his prayers. Something that worked for you and will work for him.

In the story, it's the part where you talk about 'the strange herbal tea.' He'll still be skeptical. But now you're a buddy and he's at least going to give you a shot to tell him what you've got.

But don't believe just me, you'll say. Check out what people just like you have to say about this weird concoction. And here you show him your testimonials.

But not just any testimonials. Testimonials you've sharpened like a chef's knife to cut through any remaining doubt.

Most marketers screw up testimonials. Either they don't ask for a testimonial – big mistake – or they simply copy and paste it straight into their sales letter.

Your customers haven't a clue how to write a testimonial. It's not something they learn at college. Left alone, your customer will write something like 'Love your product, man!'

That sucks! It's great they love your product but it's not going to convince anyone else to buy.

You've got to take them by the hand and show them what you're looking for. Or you've got to write it for them.

Write it for them? Isn't that cheating? Won't the FTC fall on you like a ton of bricks? Not the way smart marketers do it.

Smart marketers won't make up a testimonial. Smart marketers interview their customers to uncover what their product has done for them. And then the marketer writes the testimonial and gets the customer to sign off stating they agree with it.

Here's an example. Imagine the guy in the story above drinks the herbal tea, gets home, and phones in to order more teabags.

If you simply ask him to send in a testimonial he'll write something like 'I had a great flight after drinking your herbal tea.' Pretty dire.

But if you get him on the phone and interrogate him about the flight, you may find out the plane hit a lightning storm over Dallas and dropped 10,000 feet in 3 seconds. That for four hours the plane hit every pocket of turbulence and bounced around like a XXX. But he enjoyed every minute.

Knowing this you could write a testimonial that starts 'Flight from hell a breeze after drinking one cup of your magic tea.' It's true, of course. And he'll be happy to sign it off.

That's the end of step 1. Time for a quick review.

You start by telling your story... a story that makes your prospect think 'Me too!' Next, you reveal how you found a solution to your problem and hit your prospect with testimonials to back up your claim.

But what next?

Step 2 – Here's What I've Got For You

Next, you break down what you're offering. You don't simply say I've got an herbal tea that stops airsickness. You break it down and tell the prospect every single thing it'll do for them. And the easiest way to do it is to use bullets.

Look back at the airsickness scenario. After the guy at the bar asks "What does it do?" the next two lines are bullets.

I'll break one down to show you the structure you need to use to craft hard-hitting bullets. The first line reads "The natural plant extracts soothe the part of the brain that causes airsickness so you can sit back and relax even if the flight's as bumpy as the wildest roller-coaster."

The first part of the bullet is the feature. It's what the herbal tea does. In this case, it soothes the part of the brain that causes airsickness.

But if that's all you tell them your prospect will say 'So what! Who cares if it soothes the brain! What's in it for me?"

And that's why you hit them with the benefit "So you can sit back and relax even if the flight's as bumpy as the wildest rollercoaster."

The feature means nothing to your prospect. They can't picture their brain being soothed. Can you? But they can picture a wild roller-coaster ride in a plane... and they can picture being completely relaxed.

The trick to writing bullets is to start of breaking down the features of your product. Grab your yellow legal pad, take a fresh page, and draw a line down the middle.

On one side, at the top, write 'Features'. On the other side, write 'Benefits'.

Scribbling down features is a breeze. They're simply the physical characteristics of your product. In the airsickness story, some of the features are:

Small teabag

Orchid

Natural plant extract

Get the idea?

Now for the benefits. This is where a lot of folks – even some seasoned copywriters – struggle. But it doesn't have to be hard.

For each feature, you ask the question 'What that means to you Mr. Prospect is...' and you fill in the blanks.

Here's an example. The feature is 'natural plant extract'. What the means to you Mr. Prospect is you sit back and enjoy even the bumpiest flight. That's the benefit.

Why not have a shot at writing the benefits for the other two features?

With the features and benefits done and dusted, it's a breeze to turn them into bullets. Here's an example using the feature and benefit of the natural plant extract.

The natural plant extracts soothe the part of the brain that causes airsickness so you can sit back and relax even if the flight's as bumpy as the wildest rollercoaster.

Now you've cracked features, benefits, and bullets, it's time to explain to your prospect why he needs your product.

Step 3 - Here's Why It's Important To You

I reckon it's time for a quick recap.

In step 1 you tell your story, explain why your product is unique, and show him testimonials to prove you're not full of BS.

In step 2 you explain what your product is and how he'll benefit from it. Now it's time to...

Sell The Damn Thing!

In the airsickness story the selling begins with the line "All you do is drink the tea before you go on the flight. It's as simple as that!"

That's a pretty big promise. But the work that's been done in steps 1 and 2 makes it more believable.

What big promise can you make with your product? Does it regrow hair in 24 hours? Cure eczema in 7 days? Make them a millionaire in a year?

Grab that legal pad and write down your big promise.

But making a big promise isn't enough. Let's face it...we've all been promised something and been bitterly disappointed when it's failed.

People have been bitten on the ass so many times that making a big promise isn't enough. You've got to take away all the risk and make it easy for them to buy. It's time for the guarantee.

A lot of folks give a pretty standard guarantee. If you're not happy we'll refund all your money any time in the next 30 days. Sure, it's a guarantee, but we've seen it all before. And people are becoming immune to it.

To really grab your prospect's attention it's best if you can...

Give An Outrageous Guarantee!

Something like 'If my tonic doesn't grow back your hair in the next 24 I'll refund double your money and buy you a brand new BMW Z4. Women won't even care that you're bald when you pull up in your brand new sports car!"

Okay, that's a bit over the top but you get the idea. Are you thinking 'If I offer an outrageous guarantee, won't people take advantage of me?'

Yes, but only a handful. And the money you lose with these people will be a drop in the ocean compared to the money you'll make offering an outrageous guarantee.

But even with an outrageous guarantee most prospects will do nothing. You've got to...

Light A Fire Under His Ass!

You've got to make it more painful to sit and do nothing than it is to click the order button. You've got to shake him up and make it harder for him to buy than not to buy.

Hit him where it hurts. Push his emotional hot buttons. In the airsickness story, it's where I say...

Aren't you sick and tired of dreading every flight? Isn't it embarrassing as hell sitting next to a hot girl and spending half the flight puking into a paper bag? With this herbal tea you'll never suffer again. You'll sit back and enjoy the flight. You'll watch the movies and chat with the hot girl. Heck, you might even feel like eating the airplane food!"

And this all comes back to knowing your prospect. Knowing where he hurts and how your product can fix it.

So where have we got up to now?

In step 1 you tell your story, explain why your product is unique, and show him testimonials to prove you're not full of BS.

In step 2 you explain what your product is and how he'll benefit from it. Now it's time to...

In step 3 you show why your prospect must have this. You've got to make it easier for him to buy than not to buy.

Finally, we get to...

Step 4 – Here's What To Do Now

This is the shortest step. But the one most people screw up. You must...

Ask For The Sale!

For a lot of folks this is the hardest part. They're reluctant to ask for the sale.

That somehow nice guys don't ask for money.

That's total BS. You've got to take this thinking and rip it out of your head! If you've got a product that you believe in and that will help the prospect then don't be shy of asking for his money.

In the airsickness example, if I really believe in the herbal teabag and I know the guy will have a great flight after drinking it, isn't it the right thing to do to make him buy it.

In the story I make it easy. I say...

Here's a sample. If it doesn't do exactly what I said it does then you owe me nothing. But when it stops your airsickness, and you arrive home feeling refreshed and with more energy, then call me on 247-555-0123, give me your address and credit card details, and I'll send you a whole box for only $19.97."

I make the sale as easy as possible. I offer a free trial and then give him specific instructions how to buy more. Never assume your prospect knows what to do to buy your product. Break it down for him step by step.

First, you'll click this... then you'll see this... enter your PayPal account and click the button. Then look out for an e-mail... when it arrives click the link... etc.

Get the picture? Lead your prospect by the hand and make it a breeze to buy your product.

It's as simple as 1...2...3... Or in this case...

1. Tell your story, explain why your product is unique, and show him testimonials to prove you're not full of BS.

2. Explain what your product is and how he'll benefit from it

3. Show your prospect why he must have this. Make it easy for him to buy.

4. Ask for the sale.

That's it. The four simple steps for writing a killer sales letter.

Grab your yellow legal pad and start writing.

Colin Joss is a freelance direct response copywriter and marketing consultant. He writes sales copy that puts a .357 Magnum to your prospect's head... demands he reads every word...and forces him to hand over his hard earned money.

Trained by the world's leading copywriter, John Carlton, and by Mike Morgan, and Kevin Rogers, Colin uses Carlton's hundred million dollar 17-step copywriting blueprint to create hard-hitting copy that rakes in the big bucks. For a free consultation e-mail free@BackRoadsMarketing.com

PROVEN CONTENT: WHY YOU SHOULD BE USING PUBLIC DOMAIN WORKS TO BUILD YOUR BUSINESS

> *There ain't no rules around here. We're trying to accomplish somep'n.*
>
> — *Thomas Edison*

Tony Laidig

Let's keep this simple...if you want to make money selling information products, then you need CONTENT! And lots of it! Some have said that content is king and I completely agree! The PROBLEM has been producing that content! Think about it. You need content for your products, content for your newsletter, content for your blog, content for your articles, content for your videos... whew...that's a LOT of content! Are you up for the challenge? I wasn't, until I discovered an easy (and profitable) way to find all the content I would ever need or use.

Enter the Public Domain...

It's no secret that I'm a HUGE fan of Public Domain content, and there is a GOOD reason for that: There is simply NO other source for content on the planet that is as vast as the Public Domain ...period. Now maybe you are scratching your head wondering, "What the heck is the Public Domain?" Good question, and the answer will open up the door to a world of new opportunities for you!

The Public Domain refers to a collection of published or unpublished 'works' that are not or no longer protected by the US copyright law. The public domain inherently encompasses all creative works and other mediums of information that are not protected by copyright law. In other words, when the copyright or patent expires on a creative work (book, work of art, etc.), anyone may freely use that work LEGALLY in any manner they choose without the obligation of paying royalties to the creator of the work.

This definition gets extremely exciting when you consider that all the following are available to you right now in the Public Domain:

There are over 85 million books, many written by the greatest authors to have ever walked the earth.

There are hundreds of millions of paintings, illustrations, photographs and more produced by the world's finest artists, illustrators and photographers.

You'll find thousands of classic and current videos-all at your fingertips-from vintage movies to cartoons and documentaries.

You have full, unhindered access to the millions of reports, books, videos and images produced by our government every year at a cost of millions.

There are over 200,000 different magazine titles worth of content on practically every topic known to man.

All the patents ever issued from the beginning up until just 15 short years ago (and in some cases even sooner). That's 5.5 million patents!

Thousands of audios, recordings, radio shows, sheet music and much more!

There are hundreds of software programs of all types and for all platforms.

And SO much more!

It's honestly mind-blowing to think that there is literally THAT MUCH proven content available for you to use for product creation RIGHT NOW, and yet, chances are that you are NOT doing so!

You'll notice that I keep using the phrase "Proven Content." So much of the content that you would consider using for product creation today is either user-generated or created by a third-party (ghostwritten, PLR, interviews, etc.). The thing is that, in many cases, this type of content often has zero track record for generating sales, and in some cases, the quality of that content is less than stellar. With content from the Public Domain, you are, in many cases, working with content that has proven itself. It's already been through the editing and approval processes of publishing. It's already generated sales. It's already been read by thousands, or in some cases, hundreds of thousands of people just like you and me.

It's PROVEN itself.

This is a HUGE benefit! Why use content that is unproven when you can have access to content that has been produced by some of the brightest minds, created by geniuses and visionaries and written by the leaders and innovators of their fields of expertise?

You are beginning to understand WHY I get so excited about using Public Domain content for product creation! It truly makes SO much sense to add this powerful, transformational strategy to what you are currently doing ... online or offline!

So What Is the Public Domain?

If you want to succeed with using the proven content of the Public Domain, you have to have a basic understanding exactly what the Public Domain is.

The Public Domain refers to published or unpublished 'works' that are not protected by the U.S. Copyright law and encompasses all creative works and other mediums of information that are not protected by copyright law.

Note: 'Work' refers to anything that can possibly be published and sold including books, courses, instruction manuals, music, movies, photographs, reports, recipes, ideas, inventions and much, much more.

To understand the Public Domain, you must know how any work can potentially fall into the Public Domain. In fact, there are several ways a work can become Public Domain, and some of these are listed below:

The work was created and published before there were copyright laws. This distinction is very important and is the sole reason why the works of Shakespeare are considered Public Domain while Darwin's groundbreaking book, *Origin of Species*, is protected by copyright.

The work cannot be copyrighted. This includes things such as ideas, facts, theories, mathematical or scientific formulas, and also simple things like a list of ingredients or components. Therefore you cannot copyright the Theory of Relativity, or the knowledge of how to make a Molotov Cocktail (a type of a homemade bomb).

The work is a publication by the government, related agencies and/or officials. Specifically, the U.S. Copyright law prevents such publications from being 'copyrighted' (this has a lot to do with the definition of copyright and copyrightable work) and thus they are directly part of the public domain.

The work's copyright protection has expired (and not been renewed). If a work was published in the United States before 1923, it's in the Public Domain...period. However, if it was published between the years of 1923 and 1964, the publisher had to renew the copyright in the 28th year from publication. If the copyright was not renewed, the work fell into the Public Domain (Note: 85% to 90% of all works produced during that time frame never renewed the copyright!)

The copyright owner dedicated the work into the public domain. This is more common than you think. An often-quoted example is that of freeware software or freely distributed source code. Sometimes artists tend to dedicate their work to the Public Domain as well.

Through these methods of identity shared above, we are provided access to the largest, most vast collection of intellectual property and proven content on the planet. There are a couple sites I recommend where you can check the copyright status of books, magazines and other works. You can access them easily at this site: http://www.publicdomainblueprint.com/research/

Why are Public Domain works profitable?

The most important and exciting benefit with Public Domain works is that anyone can use them to create products of their own, either through repackaging, or from a derivative work.

Note: A derivative work is, according to copyright law, an artistic creation that includes aspects of work previously created and protected. Derivative works of copyright-protected works is prohibited by law, unless a specific permission is acquired by the author / copyright holder. Since commercial use of a work in the Public Domain is not protected by copyright law, creating a derivative work out of the Public Domain is commercially legal.

Since you are free to use information / works from the Public Domain and use them either personally or commercially without restrictions, the possibility of profiting from Public Domain works is immediate and very real.

Public Domain works are profitable because:

Many Public Domain works include (nearly) timeless and entirely relevant information on wildly popular 'interests' such as making money, self-improvement, writing, playing sports, interpreting dreams, astrology, public speaking, entrepreneurship, recipes and lots more.

The information is immediately usable – for many Public Domain works all you need is to simply do some minor editing, repackage the knowledge into a medium of your liking (we discuss this in more detail a little later) and then sell it. Of course, you can also produce derivative works, but the power of immediate reusability is one of the primary reasons many people are attracted to the public domain.

There is an abundance of such information. We're talking about publications that span over a century, and maybe even more than that when you take into account classic works that were published before copyright law even existed.

Use of a particular Public Domain work by someone else does not mean that you cannot use that same Public Domain work for your own commercial purpose. In other words, you can use the SAME Public Domain resources that someone else has used, and restructures them to suit your commercial venture. This is the real strength of the Public Domain – the information is not a resource that is 'used up' over time – in fact as more and more people begin to embrace the 'free information' movement (and the open source movement in software development), you will find that the Public Domain will only increase in size over time.

Public Domain works are in diverse mediums. You have software, books, instruction manuals, videos, audios, photographs, music and even government publications. Any and all of these mediums can be used to generate specific and different types of selling opportunities.

Public Domain works are not restricted in the format they are stored. Thus you can convert a book on interpreting dreams into an audio course, or create a website around a book on public speaking. This is more of a 'how to profit from Public Domain works' feature, but it's important enough to note here.

As it can be expected, knowing that something is profitable is not enough. You might think that finding and creating a saleable product from the Public Domain is too much work, or you may think it costs too much. You could also be worried that you don't have the right 'business experience' to pull off such a venture. Worse yet, you may think you're totally not an 'Internet' person.

These are valid fears, although completely unnecessary. In fact, Public Domain works are the best way to immediately create quick-selling products, especially if you're just starting out in setting up your business. It doesn't matter if you're particularly knowledgeable about business matters or the Internet.

How can you use Public Domain works?

As I shared earlier, using Public Domain content to help build your online or offline business provides numerous opportunities for expanding your reach into virtually any niche market. It makes so much sense to use the content in some form because it is proven and has often been produced by those who are at the top of their game! It also can explode your income in ways that you may not even be considering.

Public Domain resources are available from nearly every primary media category including books, magazines, newspapers, government materials, photographs, artwork, movies, audio recordings, ephemera and software. So let's take a look at a number of different ways you can use Public Domain works to expand your online or off-line business. Many of these methods can be used in combination with others to produce high-end packages, membership site offerings, physical products and much more. With all the options for product creation I've included here, I feel quite certain that you will find several that will fit your market, your skill set and your interest!

Republish content as-is in print form

You can easily republish Public Domain books into print for using print-on-demand technology. Scan the existing book pages to print as-is, or have the text transcribed or converted into text using OCR.

Example: *Think and Grow Rich* by Napoleon Hill has been republished dozens of times by different individuals and companies.

Republish content as-is as a downloadable e-book

Republishing Public Domain books as e-books uses the same basic techniques used for producing print versions. Scan the existing book pages as-is, or have the text transcribed or converted into text using OCR.

Example: Gutenberg.org is an online leader in moving Public Domain books into electronic form.

Republish content as-is along with other books on CD/DVD If you have ever searched for books on eBay, you have no doubt seen collections of books for sale on CD. While some vendors offer thousands of books on one CD or

DVD for a couple bucks, smart vendors are selling niche-driven collections for higher prices.

Example: B & R Samizdat (http://www.samizdat.com) provides an excellent example of what can be done (and done well) with Public Domain book collections.

Use content to develop Study Course with workbook Why not take that favorite Public Domain book and write questions or exercises for the end of each chapter or for a separate workbook or study guide? This is an excellent way to breathe new life into a classic book.

Example: A number of Public Domain self-help books such as *As a Man Thinketh* by James Allen have been enhanced in this way with great success.

Update or rewrite material for new product

In can be much easier to write or develop a new book if you have an existing foundation and Public Domain books can provide that for you. You can use this method to create new products by:

a. Updating archaic or outdated language, facts or dates

b. Using the table of contents as an outline for developing your new book

c. Rewriting the existing text so that it reflects more of your own personality

Example: Sun Tsu's *Art of War* has been rewritten into a number of excellent, updated new books, including *The Art of War for the 21st Century* by Dan Lok.

Record reading as an audio book

Using audio is a powerful way to create new products and caters to the busy lifestyle that describes many people. By reading your favorite Public Domain books, you are creating a higher value resource than by just offering the book alone. Then, you can offer the files as podcasts, as downloadable MP3s or as audio CDs...or all the above. If you have a computer and a microphone, you're set.

Example: Take the Public Domain books you are already selling and record them to use as an upsell or as a new audio-based membership site.

Use content for blog postings

How many of you have all the time in the world to write ongoing, fresh content for your blog. Imagine drawing from a relevant Public Domain resource, then copying and pasting a few paragraphs at a time to provide your readers with the content they're looking for. Public Domain books also make an excellent resource for those of you building "blogging empires" for Adsense revenue.

Example: How about taking a Public Domain recipe book and posting a new recipe every day from it on your cooking blog? This would be a great way to discover and provide fresh, "new" dishes for your readers to try on their own. Plus it builds your blog as the source for great recipes (or craft ideas, tax tips, real estate tricks, pet care ideas, success insights, etc.).

Use excerpts along with images or video to create viral movies. With the growing popularity of YouTube, Google Video and other video-share sites, the opportunities are nearly endless what can be done with Public Domain in this media. Use clips from Public Domain movies or documentaries, photographs, quotes, poems, etc. to make your own viral video to get traffic to your site.

Example: I created a video called "Power of One" where I compiled photos, music and a poem from the Public Domain that has had over 150,000 views on YouTube. I also offer the video at http://www.spiritualpublishing.com where I use it to build a list together with a book giveaway...you guessed it... also from the Public Domain.

Use poems or quotes to create t-shirts or other CaféPress-type products Websites like CafePress and Zazzle make it super easy to create physical products of all types using Public Domain works. Zazzle especially has great examples of others using this very method.

Example: Find some quotes you like and type them out in your program of choice. Upload the designs to CafePress and then sell the product on eBay. When someone purchases your product, place the order with CafePress (at your discount of course) and have it shipped directly to your customer as a gift (no packing slips that way).

Create a movie or television script from a Public Domain novel, story, or play Public Domain books, movies and plays provide wonderful source material for creating a new movie or television script based on those existing stories. Creating a new, modern version of play or musical from an original piece not only provides you with a foundation to build on for your script, but it also gives unlimited artistic freedom to shape it into your own vision for the story.

Example: The blockbuster movie, "300" is a great example of writer and director taking a story from the Public Domain—Herodotus' retelling of the battle of Thermopylae in his *Histories, Book VII*—and shaping it into a new, compelling rendition using their own artistic freedoms and creativity together with today's movie-making technologies.

Create an animated film from a Public Domain novel, story, or play There is a huge market for animated films, whether they are hand-drawn creations, 3-D computer rendered, claymation or puppet-based. Because of the constant demand for new stories, Public Domain works can provide a wealth of source material that is nearly inexhaustible.

Example: Many of Walt Disney's famous cartoons are based on fairy tales from the Public Domain including *Snow White and the Seven Dwarfs, Cinderella, Pinocchio, The Hunchback of Notre Dame, Alice in Wonderland*, and *The Jungle Book*.

Create a documentary using Public Domain photographs, art and video footage Creating content for a documentary can be a daunting task. By including content from the Public Domain, you save valuable time and also add value to your documentary by "collaborating" with many of the great photographers, artists and directors from the past.

Example: Create a documentary about fashion in the Roaring Twenties based solely on magazine covers, ads and illustrations...all from the Public Domain.

Host a film festival to show Public Domain films

There are thousands of films now in the Public Domain, many of which today's generation have never seen. Offering Public Domain films in a public format brings those classics back to life, without having to worry about public showing limitations associated with copyrighted films.

Example: Host a cartoon film festival to screen Public Domain , but also provide the opportunity for budding animators to show their talents as well.

Use Public Domain Magazine articles to create new print magazines You can easily find a number of Public Domain magazines related to your niche. Collect the best articles and republish in a new magazine with new pictures and other content.

Example: History buffs love stories related to their era of history. Create a monthly magazine of republished articles about WWII. Nothing has changed about WWII in the past 50 or so years, so the magazine content will still be relevant.

These are just a few ideas that can be put into practice quickly and easily. There are obviously many more uses for Public Domain content available to you as well. Be imaginative...be innovative...be creative...HAVE FUN!

Resources

I thought I would end this chapter by sharing some place online where you can find great Public Domain content. I've also included additional resources as well that focus on specific area of Public Domain content (and product creation) in much greater detail!

And last but not least, I also want to give you a special gift...my first book, *Public Domain Code Book*. It has sold thousands of copies and has helped many people create new businesses (or enhance existing ones). I want you to have it...for free. You will find the details of where you can download your free copy of the *Public Domain Code Book* at the end of the resources section.

Websites

Google Books (http://books.google.com)

Online Books Page (http://onlineBooks.library.upenn.edu/)

Project Gutenberg (http://www.gutenberg.org)

Library of Congress (http://www.loc.gov)

Internet Archive (http://www.archive.org)

USA Search (http://usa.gov)

Digital Book Index (http://www.digitalbookindex.com)

VisiPix (http://www.visipix.com)

Every Stock Photo (http://www.everystockphoto.com)

Wikipedia.org (http://www.wikipedia.org)

Explore More of the Public Domain

Public Domain Explained (http://www.publicdomainexplained.com) A video course that takes you in-depth into using the proven content of the Public Domain in building your online or offline business.

Easy Money Picture Project (http://www.easymoneypictureproject.com)

Drawing from my years of graphic design, publishing and photography experience, I reveal my secrets to creating profitable products using images from the Public Domain.

Limitless Blog Content (http://www.limitlessblogcontent.com) There are millions of magazine articles from nearly every niche in the Public Domain right now. And here is the BEST part...almost no one is using this powerful source for high-quality proven content. "Limitless Blog Content" shows you the secrets to tapping into this "virgin" gold mine of content and guides you around potential pitfalls.

Public Domain Profit Centers (http://www.publicdomainprofitcenters.com) PDPC reveals over 230 websites stuffed FULL of Public Domain content of all types. It also shares a wealth of in-depth insights on how to get started with the Public Domain and turn it into a profitable business model.

Create Audio Products (http://createaudioproducts.com) Audio products are the ONLY type of media that can be accessed anywhere. Your customers can't watch videos while driving or read e-books while walking the dog...but they CAN listen to audios! "Create Audio Products" shows you how to do just that...create audio products...from Public Domain content.

Get Your FREE Copy of the *Public Domain Code Book*! To get your free copy of my hugely popular book, *Public Domain Code Book*, simply go to the website (http://www.publicdomaincodebook.com), enter your name and primary e-mail address, and that's it...you'll have instant access to the e-book (originally sold for $87). You will also receive my free newsletter where I share the latest news, tips and strategies on using and profiting from the proven content of the Public Domain.

Social Tony

http://publicdomainblog.com

http://www.twitter.com/tonylaidig

http://www.faceBook.com/tonylaidig

http://www.youtube.com/kanetsv

AFFILIATE MARKETING FOR ABSOLUTE BEGINNERS

The secret to creativity is knowing how to hide your sources.

— *Albert Einstein*

Connie Ragen Green

Being able to recommend other people's products and services as an affiliate marketer has enabled me to earn a comfortable living on the Internet. I also win affiliate contests regularly, taking home prizes such as flat screen televisions, computers, iPods, and an iPad. You can do the same thing if you take some time to learn how to apply this to your online goals. It works with most any niche, so it's simply a matter of getting started.

When I came online at the end of 2005, I had no idea what I could sell in order to start making some money. It seemed like everyone already had a business before they decided to work on the Internet, and I was not a coach or someone who had previously worked in the corporate world. My background was as a classroom teacher for the previous twenty years. I had also worked in real estate during that time, taking listings and appraising houses.

None of this work experience was going to make me any money from my home computer.

I soon heard about affiliate marketing, and this resonated with me. For all of the years I had worked in real estate, referral fees were a regular part of my income. If someone was moving in or out of the area, a referral would be made between two agents and we would each earn a percentage of the commission once the deal had closed. Affiliate marketing worked on the same principles on the Internet, and I was anxious to jump in and learn more.

The first site I found out about was called Clickbank. There were more than a hundred thousand digital products available there, and each paid a generous commission. This site continues to be an excellent place to begin. I decided to purchase a dog training product and a weight loss product to see if they would be worth promoting. The decision to always purchase what I would recommend to others is one that has helped me to build my reputation online. We wouldn't recommend a restaurant we hadn't eaten at or a movie we had not seen to someone we know, so it made perfect sense to only recommend and promote what I had used personally and benefitted from on the Internet.

I started a blog for each niche and also began writing articles to submit to the article directories. I was just learning what keywords were all about, so the titles of my blog posts and article would each contain phrases that I knew people were searching for online. I used Google's free tool, the 'Keyword Tool External', to find out which phrases were searched for most often.

This was before social media, so Twitter and Facebook did not exist at that time. I believe you have at least a small advantage these days because you are able to connect with people who are interested in your topic much more quickly than in the past. I now use social media to build relationships that lead to even more affiliate sales.

During the spring of 2006 I made my first money online as an affiliate marketer. It was $21.60 from the sale of the eBook on training Yorkshire terriers. I was so excited I could hardly contain my enthusiasm! I realized that it was a small amount of money, but it represented my belief that if I could generate one sale, there were many more to come. It turned out this was only the tip of the iceberg, and that I would go on to sell many products and courses to people all over the world.

By this time I had about 50 people on my list. These people had signed up on my blog, and I was able to email them to let them know what I was doing and to answer questions about the areas I was now more knowledgeable about. Blogging and article marketing were now much easier for me, so I was able to help others get started with their online writing. At the end of 2006 I created my first product on how to write articles and blog, and three people signed up.

I took a step back at this time to evaluate my progress. I was recommending several products and courses to my list, on my blogs, and in the resource box at the end of each article I wrote and submitted. My income was increasing slowly and steadily each month, and by the end of 2006 I was making about two thousand dollars a month. The course I had just created, which took a full month of preparation and quite a bit of work, had earned me three hundred dollars in profit.

I had originally thought that affiliate marketing would only be a way for me to make money until I had my own products, but looking at the numbers showed me that this model had much more potential than I had given it credit for. I decided right then that I would continue to be an affiliate for the products and services I used and believed in, and that I would be willing to take my time in creating my own products. This was to be my plan for 2007, and I stuck to it.

2007 was a remarkable year for me. I began holding regular teleseminars to teach what I knew and to promote what I loved. Some of the people whose products and courses I was promoting allowed me to interview them for my list when they were launching a new program. I created a second product, one on using technology online, and again my affiliate sales far surpassed the sales of that program. I continued to write articles and began repurposing everything I wrote into short reports, eBooks, and outlines to use for my tele-seminars.

Soon I was able to replace the income I had made while working as a classroom teacher and in real estate six or seven days a week. This was getting better and better, and I was thrilled. Another benefit of being an affiliate for people who had been online for several years before me was that I could learn about how they ran their businesses and get a close look at their ongoing marketing strategies. This type of opportunity is priceless.

By 2008 I had begun using optin pages as a means of building my list more quickly. Social media was taking off, so I jumped in and interacted with as many people as possible. Even though I was creating 3 or 4 courses of my own at this point, I was still earning more as an affiliate marketer than from my own products and courses.

If you are just starting out as an affiliate marketing, this is what I recommend so that you can get up and running as quickly as possible. These are the 7 Steps to Success as an Affiliate Marketer:

Choose a main niche and a sub-niche. I say this because it seems like everyone prefers to have at least two areas to explore online. Resist the temptation to have more than two areas you will devote you time to because this will be plenty to keep you busy. The main niche should be an area you are willing to commit to for at least a year. Even if you do not feel like you are an expert in any area, start learning as much as you can and you will do well. I believe you can become something of an expert in about 30 days in most niches by reading and paying close attention to what is happening surrounding the niche. The sub-niche can be another area of interest for you, such as a sport or a hobby where people spend money.

Take a look at the products you have spent money on in these two areas, and become an affiliate for them. Log in to their affiliate area and see what type of tools they are providing for you, such as banner ads, tweets, and pre-written emails.

Do some keyword research with Google's free tool. It's at https://adwords. google.com/select/KeywordToolExternal, and then purchase a domain name that contains one keyword phrase, based on your research.

Create a free giveaway by writing a few pages on your topic. Don't spend too much time on this. If you find it is taking you more than a few hours to write, consider using some articles that are already published over at http://www.EzineArticles.com and just writing a few paragraphs at the beginning and end. The idea is to give people some valuable information in exchange for their name and email address and the opportunity to stay in touch with them.

Set up an optin page where you can give some information about yourself and your topic and allow people to sign up for your free giveaway. I didn't do this for the first two years I was online because I thought it would work just as well to have people sign up on my blog. I was amazed at the difference as soon as I began using optin pages. The idea is that visitors will only have two choices when they arrive at your site; they can either opt in or navigate away from your page. This system works if you offer something of value!

Write some autoresponder messages that will go out automatically to the people who sign up to be on your list. Remember that they are most interested when they first opt in, so be sure to contact them regularly for the first couple of weeks. These email messages must contain valuable content on your niche topic, links to relevant blog posts and articles you have written, and offers for them to purchase the products you are recommending.

Now you will want to drive targeted traffic to your optin page in order to build your list. You can do this by blogging, writing articles and submitting them to the article directories, setting up a group or a fan page on Facebook, connecting with people on Twitter, posting to forums, writing short reports, creating audio recordings and videos, and holding regular teleseminars.

My list is still relatively small, but the people who stay with me are very responsive. This means that you do not need a list of ten thousand names to begin making money online; you just need a list of people who are interested in what you have to say and are willing to spend money on what you are recommending to them. Remember to be a problem solver throughout this entire process. By answering the questions and solving the problems of your target market, they are more likely to join and remain on your list, as well as purchase information from you.

These 7 steps will help you to lay the foundation of an online business based on affiliate marketing. Think of yourself as the person who will recommend only the best products, courses, and services to the people who come to you for advice and information in your niche. You will begin to build your credibility in your field, and people will trust you more and more. You will also gain more visibility as you continue to create content and interact on teleseminars and in social media settings.

In the four and a half years that I have now been working exclusively online I have seen many changes. I have also grown as an entrepreneur and a marketer. The only thing that remains the same is my enthusiasm with recommending and promoting other people's products as an affiliate marketer.

Connie Ragen Green is a list relationship marketer who helps new online entrepreneurs to build a profitable business by connecting with others who are interested in their area of expertise. She specializes in helping people make huge profits with even a tiny list. Connect with Connie by visiting her site at http://HugeProfitsTinyList.com.

ARISTOTLE'S BOOTY,
OR, HOW TO GET PEOPLE TO BUY ANYTHING

Dr. Joe Vitale

How do you sell a T-shirt, anyway?

I mean, nobody really needs one. Many places give them away as promotional items. And there isn't a shortage of them in the world. They aren't food, water, or shelter. They aren't essential. No one will die without one.

So why would anyone buy one of mine?

Those were the thoughts I wrestled with after artist Andy Dooley created a beautiful T-shirt design to celebrate my book, *Spiritual Marketing*, becoming a number one best-seller on Amazon June 4th and 5th, 2002.

Now that I have a shirt, how do I sell it?

I rummaged through my brain as well as my library and stumbled across Aristotle. You may remember him. He was an ancient Greek rhetorician who created a four-point system for persuasion. That system has never been improved on in the last 2,000 years. In brief, his logical 4-step "arrangement" (as Aristotle called it) looks like this:

1. Exordium. A shocking statement or story to get attention.

2. Narratio. You pose the problem the reader/listener is having.

3. Confirmatio. You offer a solution to the problem.

4. Peroratio. You state the benefits of action on the solution.

This should look a little familiar to you. It's very similar to the classic advertising formula known as AIDA: Attention, Interest, Desire, Action.

Because of both of those formulas, most of my sales oriented writing follows along the easy path of answering these questions:

1. Are you getting attention with your opening?

2. Are you stating a problem the reader cares about?

3. Are you offering a solution that really works?

4. Are you asking the reader to take action?

Okay. You got that. But how does it help me sell T-shirts?

Well, let's see.

1. My opening has to grab attention. So what if I said something like, "How can you wear a painting that will increase your sex appeal?" Food, sex, and money are notorious attention-getters.

2. Now I have to state a problem. So maybe I can ask, "Are you tired of wearing ratty T-shirts from the local pub or grill? Wouldn't you like to wear something that makes you feel great---that reminds you---as well as the people who are attracted to you---to go for your dreams?"

3. Now I have to explain my solution. "Famous artist Andy Dooley, who has designed T-shirts sold at Disney World and around the world, has just created an original work of art. This art is beautiful, colorful, and charged with the feelings that attract prosperity, love, and healing---all the things you loved in the book, *Spiritual Marketing*."

4. To wrap up, I need to now ask for action. "You can only get this limited-edition, original work of art directly from me. Just see my website at http://www.mrfire.com and you'll see the T-shirt design. For every 3 shirts you buy, I'll send you one free. Sizes are Large and X-Large only."

Wow! I did it!

I spontaneously created a sales piece by following Aristotle's 2,400 year-old 4-step plan.

You can do this, too. For anything you want to sell, simply ask yourself these questions:

1. Are you getting attention with your opening?

2. Are you stating a problem the reader cares about?

3. Are you offering a solution that really works?

4. Are you asking the reader to take action?

Now go and make Aristotle proud!

Dr. Joe Vitale is famous for creating Hypnotic Writing and Miracles Coaching, but he's also written 53 books (such as *The Attractor Factor*), appeared in 13 movies (such as the hit *The Secret*), and has bestselling audios (such as *The*

Secret to Attracting Money) and more. His main website is http://www.joevitale.com. Read his book *Attract Money Now* for free at http://www.attractmoneynow.com

YOUR INNER GAME

To be yourself in a world that is doing its best, day and night to make you like everybody else --- is to fight the hardest battle any human being can fight; and never stop fighting.

— *e. e. cummings*

Pat O'Bryan

I've found that until you get your "inner game" together, your outer game just won't work.

What is your inner game?

It's the voices your hear in your head. Your self-talk.

If you're walking a tight-rope over a deep canyon, and the voices in your head are telling you: "you're going to fall! Look down! See how far it is! You're going to fall!"

You're going to fall.

However, if the dialog inside your head is more like: "Wow, this is easy. Lots of people have walked this rope before, and I can do it, too. It's almost too easy. Wonder what's for diner ..."

You'll be safely on the other side before you know it.

Your goal is to become your own best friend.

A regular meditation practice will help. You can meditate no matter what Religion you practice, even if your choice is "none of the above." In addition to helping you master your mind, meditation has proven physical benefits.

There are some good meditation audios at http://meditateforsuccess.com

I also recommend using affirmations. The idea is to replace the negative self-talk with positive self-talk. You can make this a habit, and it will help you in many ways. Relationships get better. You fearlessly try business ideas that previously would have scared you. You get luckier and better looking.

Well, I can't guarantee the last one, but it's worked for me.

Using affirmations can be as simple as sitting in a comfortable chair and either silently or out loud repeating the affirmations over and over again. Breathe. Repeat the affirmation with each breath.

One of the easiest and most powerful affirmations is "I like myself."

One my grandmother used was "day by day in every way I'm getting better and better."

You can find lists of positive affirmations online. Use the ones that resonate with you.

If you'd like some help with affirmations, and enjoy nice, soothing music, check out the Clearing Audios at http://milagroresearchinstitute.com.

Dr. Joe Vitale and I developed those to make the inner game work easy for you. And fast.

The bigger picture on the inner game is this: most people spend their entire lives at the bottom of Maslow's Hierarchy. Foraging for shelter and food. Survival.

The value of the Portable Empire System is that it frees you up from having to waste your time on survival, so you can play around at the top of the pyramid. Up there you'll find creative past-times, self-actualization, and the things that make life worth living.

I recommend spending as much time as you can up there. Life is short. You may have a philosophy that addresses what happens after you die, but you don't really know. It's possible that this is it.

One of my favorite Buddhist sayings is, "The fact of your death is known. The time of your death is unknown. What, then, shall you do?"

Every moment is precious. By developing your inner game, you'll have the tools to squeeze the juice out each moment - in the moment.

Living In The Real World: Right Here, Right Now

Our individuality is all, all that we have. There are those
who would barter it for security, but blessed in the twinkle

of the morning star is the one who nurtures and rides it, in grace and love and wit.

— *Tom Robbins*

One of the most powerful inner game strategies I've found so far is "Loving What Is." Yes, I know that's the title of a Byron Katie book. It works.

Another of her sayings is, "Don't argue with reality. You'll lose."

What's interesting to me is how clearly this ties in with my studies of Buddhism and Taoism.

Here it is in a nutshell: things happen. For example, the week before I was going to drive from Texas to Las Vegas, NV, I had a fender-bender accident in a parking lot in Austin. Bummer.

That meant that I had to take my Volvo to Las Vegas instead of my new 4Runner. The new 4Runner is much cooler (to me) and has a much superior sound system, which is important when you're driving 12 hours a day.

So, I found myself saying, "I wish I hadn't had that stupid accident..."

Tough. It happened. Once it happened, wishing wasn't going to change it.

Regret and guilt are mind-killers. And yet, we spend, sometimes, years wishing that something in the past hadn't happened. We tell ourselves, "if only..." and imagine what we would have done or said differently.

Here's the good news, and it will clear up a lot of mind-space and help you stay in the moment. The faster you can go from something happening to accepting that it happened, the better off you will be.

The "inner game" work is skipping right over "I wish" and going to "it is" as quickly as possibly. Then, your mind is free to deal with the world as it actually is without wasting time and band-width on fantasy and wishes.

This is also what the Buddha was talking about when he discussed desire. It's fine to desire abundance. However, Buddha was adamant about being in the moment and living in a state of reality.

It's one thing to look at a nice house and want it, as long as you then develop strategies for actually getting it and implement those strategies.

It's quite another to look at a nice house and want it, and then wish for it, feel bad because you don't have it, think about things you might have done in the past that would lead to you having it now, or imagining fantasies that might lead you to have it in the future. The second option can lead to grief, regret, and useless desire. This is a distraction that can keep you from leading a happy life, and from doing those things that will lead to a happy life.

Fantasy, wishes, guilt and regret- those are the components of depression. I know. Learning this simple strategy will help you skate right over the black holes of depression and get to the next action step.

Do it. You'll feel better, and you'll get a lot more done.

USE THE CLEARING AUDIOS TO
SUPERCHARGE YOUR INNER GAME

The reason visualization is so powerful is because as you create pictures in your mind of seeing yourself with what it is you want, you are generating thoughts and feelings of having it now. Visualization is simply powerfully focused thought in pictures, and it causes equally powerful feelings.
— *Rhonda Byrne*

You probably know that I teach that you have to have your inner game and your outer game both rocking if you want to accomplish anything interesting.

Your outer game is the stuff you do. I'm an author and Internet marketer, so my outer game involves creating content for the web, writing articles and books and blogs (these first two overlap a great deal), and creating the matrix that starts with interesting content and leads to people buying my products. Autoresponders, advertising, social networking, shopping carts, affiliates (more on that soon), and domains, hosting, and web pages... these are all part of my outer game.

Your inner game is the architecture of your mind. For example, the first place most people need to start their inner game work is with their internal dialog. The things you say when you talk to yourself.

One quick, easy and effective way to replace your current self-talk with more positive self-talk is to use Clearing Audios. You can find them at the Milagro Research Institute website, http://MilagroResearchInstitute.com.

Each of these audios is designed to address a specific problem you are having: money, relationships, happiness, except the original Clearing Audio, which is designed to get you started by replacing the most common negative self-talk with positive self-talk. I recommend you start with the original

Clearing Audio.

These audios come with three different mixes:

1. Music with affirmations you can hear and binaural beats. Binaural beats are a very cool technology that automatically causes your brain to entrain with two slightly out-of-tune frequencies. This will lead your brain to the state best suited to metabolize the affirmations. It's a very powerful technology and requires quite a bit of research before you can get it right. I've been working with them for seven years now and I'm pretty good at designing them.

2. Music with affirmations you can't hear (subliminal), plus binaural beats. There is a lot of disagreement about whether subliminal affirmations work or not. I've got a lot of emails from customers who use our audios that claim they do. Also, large corporations and big-box stores use them embedded in their muzak to cut down on theft and encourage buying. Right now, the evidence shows that they work.

3. Just the music.

Here's the best way to use those audios.

1. Listen to the first one- the one with the affirmations you can hear- until you can anticipate the affirmation. Think of it like singing along with a song you know. The first time you heard "Let It Be," you couldn't sing along with it. If you're anywhere near my age- even if you're not- I'll bet you can sing along with Paul all the way through the song. Once you know the first track well enough to say the affirmations along with Joe, you're ready to move on to #2.

2. Listen to the second one and say the affirmations. It's probably best to say them out loud, but just saying them silently to yourself will work, too. After you're comfy with this, you're ready for #3.

3. Listen to just the music. In the same way that an instrumental version of "Let It Be" will trigger the lyrics in our minds, the Clearing Music will trigger the affirmations.

You can keep the music going in the background while you're working, reading, surfing the web... and your mind will be filled with positive, clearing affirmations. More importantly, those negative affirmations that you may have had before: "I can't do it," "I don't deserve it," "nothing good ever happens to me," etc. will be driven out of your mind by the positive affirmations.

This is good.

It's the secret to my success, and every successful person I know uses some form of this technology, and that includes NFL football players, Olympic athletes, and business superstars. Internet Marketers including many you would be surprised at- use binaural beats and affirmations religiously.

I recommend that you start with the original Clearing Audio and use it until you have it completely metabolized. Then, go to the Milagro Research Institute website and find the next audio that addresses the problem you want to solve next and work with that one. I recommend using them one at a time, which is what I told the person who called me on the office phone. She wanted to buy a bunch of them and get Clear immediately.

It doesn't work that way.

Think of it like working out (except more fun and less strenuous.) If you immediately go to the advanced physical workout stuff, you'll be sore and frustrated. You will then stop going to the gym. You need to start where you are and work up to the more advanced stuff. By the time you're ready for the Advanced Clearing Audio, for example, you need to be ready for it. Don't start there.

WHAT NEXT?

Forget your perfect offering. There is a crack in everything.
That's how the light gets in.

— Leonard Cohen

Congratulations!

If you've read this far, and most won't, you've completed a full Internet Marketing course and gathered some very valuable inner game strategies..

Like I mentioned in my foreword, this is a book you DO. If you've done this book, you're probably well on your way to making money. If you just read the book- that won't help. Now that you know what to do, you have to actually do it.

I'll be watching.

Initially, you can run your Portable Empire for free. PayPal, blogger, and services like Clickbank don't charge for you to use them, and they make a fine starting place.

Later, you'll want an autoresponder, shopping cart, and other tools. These are not free, but they are essential as you ramp up your business. I keep a list of these resources online at http://patobryan.com/tools, and I update it as I find new cool stuff. Some of these resources are also free. Check there often.

Although this book is a complete Internet Marketing course, you may want more help. The Portable Empire Coaching program is your next step. It's at http://portableempirecoaching.com

I designed that coaching program to accelerate your success. You get time with me- not an assistant- and you get access to my video library, Camtasia videos that will teach you - step by step - how to do what you need to do, and mastermind and networking opportunities with me and the other students. It works.

I've developed solutions for you - grab them as you need them. They're at http://www.patobryan.com/products.html

Several times in this book I mention Your Inner Game. Dr. Joe Vitale and I have developed some pretty amazing resources for you to jump start your development in this area. They're at http://milagroresearchinstitute.com.

I post new ideas and research as I discover it on my blog at http://patobryan.com/blog. Check there at least once a week to see the new stuff.

And- it can be a lonely old world. Once or twice a year I host UnSeminars, which are a combination of an Internet Marketing Seminar and a gathering of the tribe. Once you get into Internet Marketing, you'll discover that it's hard to explain what you're doing. Your friends and your family will look at you strangely.

Until you start bringing in the money.

But, even then, although they're much more accepting of your new lifestyle, they probably won't understand it unless they actually do it.

At UnSeminars, you'll be surrounded by people who are living like you: free, mobile, and making cash online. It feels good. Watch my blog for announcements. This is something you want to do.

BACKWORD

The person who risks nothing, does nothing, has nothing,
is nothing, and becomes nothing. He may avoid suffering
and sorrow, but he simply cannot learn and feel and
change and grow and love and live.

— *Leo F. Buscaglia*

The place where most people get tripped up is here: They find it hard to believe it's as easy as it looks. That keeps them from doing it.

Trust me. This is exactly as easy as it looks.

You need someone to sell to and something to sell them. Your job is to help people. Find their problems and solve them. They will reward you handsomely.

So gather your tools, keep working on your "inner game," and go forth and claim your freedom: financial freedom, spiritual freedom, freedom of mobility, and just plain freedom. It's yours if you want it.

Good luck!

RESOURCES

Pat O'Bryan - let's stay in touch! http://patobryan.com

You'll want to watch my blog. That's where I post articles and musings about life, Internet Marketing, and inner game adventures.

Pat's Blog: http://patobryan.com/blog

Talk to me! You especially want to join me on Facebook. That's where I post my latest information in real time.

Facebook: http://facebook.com/pat.obryan

Twitter: http://twitter.com/patobryan

When you're ready to kick it into overdrive, you're ready for Pat's Coaching Program. When you join you'll immediately get access to:

- Videos from UnSeminars featuring Dr. Joe Vitale, Marlon Sanders, Wendi Friesen, Connie Green, Tony Laidig and dozens more teaching you everything from copywriting to inner game strategies. You can watch these videos any time you like.
- Training videos that will show you the tech stuff you need to be successful. How to build a web page, set up your autoresponder, build a squeeze page, and get the money.
- You'll want to participate in the weekly webinars where I do training and answer questions live.
- You'll be part of a mastermind group, which can be the most powerful part of your business success.
- You'll have access to the main forum, where all the coaching students hang out, help each other, and set up Jvs, co-writes, etc.

Go to http://portableempirecoaching.com and sign up now!

Clearing Audios - these are important tools you can use anywhere to get amazing results fast at the Milagro Research Institute.

Milagro Research Institute: http://milagroresearchinstitute.com

Internet Marketing resources: Pat's products, including his latest tricks and strategies, are at http://patobryan.com/products.html

You'll need an autoresponder.

ßPat recommends Aweber: http://pat.aweber.com

You may want a shopping cart. Pat uses 1ShoppingCart. They also have an autoresponder. http://bit.ly/hithzD

Pat keeps a list of free, cheap and useful tools – check 'em out.

Tools: http://patobryan.com/tools

www.ingramcontent.com/pod-product-compliance
Lightning Source LLC
Chambersburg PA
CBHW061318220326
41599CB00026B/4930